LIFE WORK PLANNING

LIFE
WORK
PLANNING

Arthur G. Kirn, Ph.D.
Marie O'Donahoe Kirn, A.M.

Life Work Planning Associates

Fourth Edition

McGraw-Hill Book Company

*New York   St. Louis   San Francisco   Auckland   Bogotá   Düsseldorf
Johannesburg   London   Madrid   Mexico   Montreal   New Delhi
Panama   Paris   São Paulo   Singapore   Sydney   Tokyo   Toronto*

This book was set in Helvetica by Kingsport Press, Inc.
The editors were Robert G. Manley, Michael LaBarbera, and Irene Curran;
the designer was Anne Canevari Green;
the production supervisor was Angela Kardovich.
The illustrations were done by Dale Saltzman.
Edwards Brothers Incorporated was printer and binder.

LIFE
WORK
PLANNING

Library of Congress Cataloging in Publication Data

Kirn, Arthur G   date
    Life work planning.

    Bibliography: p.
    1. Group relations training. I. Kirn, Marie
O'Donahoe, joint author. II. Title.
HM134.K57 1978   301.11   77-16086
ISBN 0-07-034835-9

So many are here . . .

   . . .   Peg and Jim Vaughan, Sam Deep, Ed Cyphers, Jackie Horn, Charlie Koppelman, Jim Wetzig, University Associates—our early history.

   . . .   Training Associates and members whose continuing commitment keeps us moving.

   . . .   The great number of participants who have grown and have passed the word.

   . . .   Jack Gibb, Elisabeth Kübler-Ross, Chuck Kepner, Ben Tregoe, Sid Simon, Herb Shepard, Abe Maslow, Peter Drucker, George Prince, Herbert Otto, and others who are in these pages.

   . . .   Remarkable Helen Ring.

   . . .   Dale Saltzman—he understands.

   . . .   Josh and Sarah—who so often cut through the hassle and show us who we are.

Contents

PHASE II
PUTTING IT ALL TOGETHER

APPENDIX

Preface

Change is everywhere these days—within us, in those around us, in our personal circumstances, and in a complex world that touches each of us. The Life Work Planning experience offers a process of engaging change, a process that enables *you* to find your ways of initiating change and of dealing with change initiated by others. Life Work Planning reflects our personal convictions about ourselves and about change, convictions which have evolved through the many changes in our own lives and through contact with thousands of persons who, like us, have struggled to make change work *for* them.

We state these convictions briefly here. You will meet them again in your own experience with the activities of Life Work Planning.

- We can know who we are enough to act out of our own values, needs, and interests. There is a core self that lies beneath circumstances, relationships, and activities. We tend to get so caught up in role playing and in meeting the needs of others that we lose touch with that deep self—with our strengths, ideals, and fears. We can become that self.

- We can choose to trust. Jack Gibb, in a distinguished career of psychological research and work with groups, now applies to organizational management his radical theory that all human behavior can be placed on a fear-trust continuum. At every moment we can choose to trust ourselves, trust others, trust the situation—or we can choose to fear the same. Anxiety can quickly become excitement if we make the rational choice not to be afraid of failure and attack but to trust ourselves and the situation which lies ahead. You can make that choice for yourself right now!

- It is a mark of our humanness—of our human nature—to take responsibility for our choices, behavior, and feelings. We may not always be proud of our actions or pleased with the outcome. But until we "own" our behavior and feelings, we cannot move beyond them. No one else makes us angry, loving, or happy—*we* make the choice to feel that way. Only if we accept the effects of our own choices, behavior, and feelings are we free to deal with those effects. Our young children are learning that it is their authenticity that brings joy to their lives—that joy is not our gift to them—and that it is their striking out at others which brings the hurt back to them. Trusting others to take responsibility for themselves frees relationship from dependence. How easy it is to feel responsible for someone else's pain, joy, or fear—and in taking it upon ourselves, we don't respect their capacity to take responsibility for their own lives! How easy it is to try to help, creating dependence upon ourselves, rather than to build relationship out of which a mutually helpful interdependence is possible. Each of us is strong enough to bear the burden as well as the delight of our own actions—we must let each other live our lives.

- About 95 percent of the human race lives on 5 percent of its potential. Many authorities have said this—with different percentage points and in different styles—Abe Maslow, Herbert Otto, Gordon Allport, Gardner Murphy, Carl Rogers, and Margaret Mead.

  We discover, in moments of stress or high energy, that we can do things we never dreamed we could do. Resources and strengths that have never been tested become real forces; assumed limitations lose their power. To get in touch with our potential is as confronting as it is exhilarating—we feel guilty about our unused selves and overwhelmed by glimpses of what might have been. Life takes on new zest, though, when we dare to challenge the potential within us and to push beyond the limits for which we have settled.

- To change is to risk. Change is a giving up of what we know to move into the unknown. There is always the risk of failure, hurt, rejection, and loneliness. While we more easily take a risk in a situation of trust, it often takes an initial risk to begin the process of building that trust. Someone must begin the process.

- We cannot deal effectively with any one change in isolation from our broader experience—relationships, situations, events, and our total lifetime. Each change has impact on other parts of our lives, and the more total picture lends perspective to specific decisions. Career-choice and life-style decisions interconnect.

- In any change we are not free to take on the new until we have let go of the old. This is true of major changes, such as one's job, location, or marriage, and also of minor changes, like a new butcher at your meat counter or a new toothpaste. In her work with the experience of death, life's final change, Elisabeth Kübler-Ross has identified what appear to be the classic stages in the process of letting go. Acceptance may come slowly. We naturally move through denial, anger, bargaining, and grief on the way. Just like the dying patient, we may get stuck—we deny the reality, we feed our anger, we negotiate unrealistic bargains, we nurture our grief or depression. Once they have moved through these stages, people die with confidence and in peace. Once we have accepted our loss in any of life's changes, we are free to live; and we have also taken a step toward acceptance of our own death. In this light, resistance to change can be seen as part of the natural process of letting go that has to occur if we are ever to accept the new in our lives.

• Finally, we value the importance of thinking things through—of gathering the evidence and weighing it carefully—when the hunch is not enough. Using our heads is a natural and necessary complement to getting in touch with our feelings and inclinations.

It has been an exciting and often discouraging struggle for us to get in touch with the feelings we had been afraid to admit or to feel. We now know ourselves better and like ourselves better. We delight in our increasing trust in our hunches and our intuition. We value the self-awareness which lends meaning and depth to every decision or plan. But until self-awareness at every level joins with awareness of the circumstances and conditions of our reality, and until all this awareness is submitted in some orderly way to our practical good judgment, the process of dealing with change out of our whole self is not complete. Phase II of Life Work Planning reflects this concern.

Life Work Planning is a very practical experience. You will be concerned with *your* life and work and will explore both in a structured and closely timed series of activities. You will work at a depth which is comfortable for you. You will work on those issues which are of most concern to you.

Phase I, in a sequence from past to future, offers you an opportunity to get in touch with your own self, to explore your experiences and your values and to better understand the basis for choice in your life. No one can do this for you, but sharing the process with others can be a powerful asset in your own exploration. You will work throughout Phase I in a small subgroup with alone time to develop and record your perceptions as well as some time to share experiences with your total group or class.

We have included in Phase I several articles which offer some theoretical observations on, and suggestions for, your experience of the activities. Each of these articles is identified by a small symbol, above the title. You may wish to read these sections when they appear in the program sequence. You may find it more satisfactory to read these theory sections outside of your work sessions and to use them for reflection upon your experience.

At the end of Phase I you will summarize what you know about yourself in order to set objectives and action steps for the future. In Phase II you will work with specific tools to analyse, plan, make decisions, and create new ideas for problem areas. The shift from the subjective exploration of your experience and feelings to this more objective and rational analysis of your situation may be difficult, but Phase II will enable you to complete this Life Work Planning experience with some realistic and practical action in mind.

This program is an introduction to the process of Life Work Planning. It provides an opportunity to engage the situation in which you find yourself today. You will meet many change situations and points of choice in your lifetime. Many people have found it useful to return to the process and to use any or all of the tools as new situations arise. We hope that Life Work Planning will serve you well in the years ahead.

Arthur G. Kirn
Marie O'Donahoe Kirn

Comments for groups without a leader

We hope that the directions for each activity are complete enough that you will have no trouble taking yourselves through the program. There are points, however, which might be useful to know before you begin Life Work Planning.

GROUPING

We feel that the optimal size of a working group is four or five. This number seems to suit both the need for sharing with others and for feedback from them—as well as the need to move the program along at a reasonable pace. Two or three will work, but there will be less experience to share. In a group of more than five persons, activities will take too long a time or each individual will have much less time.

If you have six or seven in your group, you may wish to break into subgroups; but use the larger group for activities which would profit from more feedback. At eight persons, you have an obvious break point for two subgroups.

A single small group tends to ignore time constraints more easily than a larger group broken down into working subgroups. If you are one small group, be sure to observe the suggested time limits.

Give some thought to the makeup of your group. You will be sharing a lot of yourself and looking to the others for important feedback. Try to choose people with whom you can share and work productively. Those with whom you feel most comfortable may or may not be those with whom it is most productive for you to work. Take the responsibility to make a choice that is good for you, even where that involves some risk.

TIME

The complete program takes about 25 hours for a group of four or five persons. Fewer persons will take relatively less time. While any of the activities in Life Work Planning will give you some useful insights, the flow of the complete design, including use of the Phase II activities, will give you a much more productive experience. Whatever time frame you establish for your experience, we hope that you will commit yourselves to that total of 25 hours.

There does not seem to be a single, proven, best time schedule for Life Work Planning. You may work through several full days, or you may plan shorter sessions, of two hours or more each, spread over a longer period of time. Straight time has the advantage of concentration, intensity, and unity. It calls up energy reserves people seem willing and happy to expend. Split time gives everyone the opportunity to absorb and reflect between sessions, and it allows for some preparation to be done outside the actual sessions. The trade-offs seem about equal.

It is important to stress that outside interruptions can be very disruptive. If you miss an activity, you lose some of the continuity and flow. In addition, you hamper the work of your group, which depends on you for interaction and feedback.

Life Work Planning is a tightly structured, task-oriented design that works. Open-ended encounter is a perfectly valid personal growth experience, but Life Work Planning is not that. The activities in this program have been designed and organized on a tight time schedule to aid you in achieving some very specific results. In choosing to engage in this process, you are taking on an established and proven dynamic. We urge you to stick to it!

Each activity has its own suggested time estimate. In many activities, you will be tempted to go on beyond our suggested deadline. The time limitation may seem obtrusive and arbitrary on those occasions. We have found that if something is of real significance, it will come up again and again, each time from a different point of view. Nothing will be lost if you do not take the time to fully work something through at any one point. So get a timer and try to follow a time schedule that has proved effective for thousands of participants. Be sure to allow time beyond working time for getting started, for breaks, for digressions, for fooling around, and for other worthwhile distractions.

MATERIALS

This workbook includes work sheets for most activities, but you will want to use a very large sheet of paper (easel pad, newsprint, or a large paper shopping bag cut open) for several activities. You will also need felt pens in many colors or crayons (which are more difficult to use and less colorful) in these activities. "Who Am I?" requires 15 small (3- by 5-inch) sheets of paper for each of you. "What Do You See?" suggests the use of a major daily newspaper or news magazine; *The New York Times* has been most useful to us, but you may find others more available and appropriate.

You will need pens or pencils as well. A kitchen timer is a great aid in keeping time. Masking tape will help to post drawings and lists on the walls or doors; we find it stimulating to have them visible to the entire group.

And don't forget refreshments. You will find some relief from the intensity of your work in an occasional cup of tea or coffee or a glass of soda, beer, or wine!

PLACE/SPACE

We suggest using a single room that is large enough so that all of you can meet together comfortably and each of you can work alone with some floor or table space.

Beyond that, our first recommendation is that the room be as interruption-free and as private as possible. A rug makes sitting on the floor more comfortable. Chairs may be useful, but they must be movable. We strongly recommend that you do *not* sit around a table. Informality and comfort set the tone for building trusting and productive relationships.

EMOTIONAL STRESS

Life Work Planning is an intense and moving experience. Along with its fun and hard work may come very powerful feelings. For most participants, this is significant, stimulating, sometimes grief-provoking, but not overwhelming. The best resource for dealing with strong feelings will be the warmth and support of a group of people who are all sharing the same experience.

If a participant's feelings do cause real distress, withdrawal from the experience may seem the wisest step. In that case, we would suggest finding someone with whom the individual can work on the distressing feelings in order to develop the capacity to live with them or to move beyond them.

Follow the instructions. Rely on your timer. Trust each other. Have a good time!

Arthur G. Kirn
Marie O'Donahoe Kirn

LIFE WORK PLANNING

Finding out about your work and life

Statement of your life work situation

WHERE ARE YOU?

30 minutes

The first step in Life Work Planning is to give some attention to your present situation, to the point at which you begin the process of planning ahead.

1. Take 10 minutes now to fill out the questionnaire below. Give some real thought to the questions, but make your answers brief and to the point. You will be asked to share this information with the group.

Briefly describe your life work situation: your work—what you do, your job, occupation, work experience, studies, how you make a living; and your life—how you live, your life style, the quality of your life.

_____

_____

_____

_____

What concerns you now? Your life? Your work? Both?_____

_____

Why?_____ _____

_____

_____

What is changing in your life and work? How?

You?_____

_____

Your work?_____

_____

Your life?_____

_____

If you are under pressure to do anything about your life or work situation, or both, what is it and when do you have to do it?

_____

_____

Is your priority concern in the workshop:
☐ To increase your self-awareness regarding work and life?
☐ To sort out alternatives and make a choice?
☐ To plan to meet a goal you have already set?
☐ To test a goal or direction before planning?
☐ To generate new alternatives, actions, or solutions?

☐ Other_____

_____

_____

2. When you have filled out the questionnaire, share your life work situation with your group using the following procedure:

Based on your answers above, make a brief statement of (a) how you see your present life work situation, (b) whether your focus is life, work, or both, and (c) what you expect to get out of Life Work Planning. (*A few minutes per person*)

Try to limit your statement to these three questions. Avoid rambling life histories and lengthy stories of the "let me fill you in on the background'.' type; this tends to get heavy, too involved, or boring, and it takes too much time. But do not be too cursory and limited; that will not give your group a clear picture of each situation and will set a tone that lacks spontaneity and feeling.

You may find that you are a little fuzzy about defining your situation now. This may be why you are here—to clarify things. Phase I will be an in-depth exploration of yourself and of your present circumstances that should help you to see your situation clearly.

The last question anticipates Phase II, when you will move from the present to make choices and establish plans for the future. The exploration of yourself in Phase I will be of practical value only as you put what you discover to work for you in Phase II.

You or your colleagues may find this to be a new experience. You may find some anxiety in the group or feel anxious yourself. You or others may face very difficult situations in your lives. Do not expect to resolve things now. Be sensitive to each other but do not get drawn into helping or problem solving. Listen, accept, support, and move on. The entire program is designed to deal with these situations. This first activity is intended simply to present them.

By asking group members to speak in random order, you capitalize on natural parallels among your respective situations. Budget your time so that each of you has a fair share. Be sure to listen to the statements of others.

Who would like to be first?

Introductory activities

TRUST AND BEGIN

These first three activities will introduce you to each other and to some of the themes and dynamics of Life Work Planning. We would like you to understand from these exercises that you can learn from your own experience—rather than from information given by a "teacher" or "leader." We will raise a series of questions. We hope that you will see what it is to be responsible for your own replies and your own self rather than to depend on what someone else thinks of them. We will set some norms of open communication—that is, we will seek to achieve trust, self-disclosure, feedback, listening, experiment, play, risk, and respect for others.

1. Below is a long list of questions which opens up a wide range of topics reflecting the comprehensive scope of the workshop. Answering these questions for yourself is a quick way to raise many concerns and to encourage you to identify—and to take responsibility for—your values and choices. Sharing some of your answers with your group is a simple way to get to know those with whom you are sharing the Life Work Planning experience and to get some sense of who you are as a group. It may surprise you to see how

many differences there are among the members of the group; or you may find yourself surprised at how alike your experience and values seem to be to those of others. (*15 minutes*)

Each question asks you to take a stand on a given subject. Do you or don't you? Would you or wouldn't you? Have you or haven't you? Are you for or against? Yes or no? Indicate your response in the appropriate column.

You may find yourself tempted to answer some of the questions both "yes" and "no." Try to resist this and to take a stand one way or the other. The point is not to be "right" but to clarify your choice of values. Forcing your response may seem a bit artificial, but if you are confused or ambivalent, trying out one position to see how it feels often clarifies your real choice. As you go through the list, check off the questions you would like to ask your group.

	Yes	No
Do you take regular exercise?		
Do you enjoy time off from work better than work?		
Do you think it is important to go to church?		
Have you taken time this autumn to watch the leaves fall (or this winter to watch the snow fall, or this spring to watch the rain fall, or this summer to watch the stars)?		
Have you read a book in the last year?		
Have you read a book in the last month?		
Have you ever smoked pot?		
Do you usually have a drink before dinner?		
Have you ever been fired?		
Have you ever quit a job?		
Do you sometimes think of dying or what death may be like?		
Are you afraid of death?		
Do you ever cry at movies or while watching television?		
Do you feel strongly about some religion or religious beliefs?		
Do you watch television more than two hours a day on the average?		

	Yes	No
Are you politically active—i.e., do you actively support some political cause?		
Have you ever written to your representative in Congress?		
Do you know your federal representative's name?		
Do you believe in love at first sight?		
Do you have a satisfying, intimate relationship with another person?		
Do you have a satisfying sexual relationship with another person?		
Do you live way out in the country?		
Do you live in the suburbs?		
Do you live in the inner city?		
Do you like where you live?		
Do you like to travel?		
Do you travel as much as you would like?		
Have you traveled outside the United States?		
Do you believe in marriage?		
Do you live alone?		
Do you enjoy being alone?		
Do you have enough time to be alone?		
Are you ever lonely?		
Do you find it hard to trust strangers?		
Do you make close friends easily?		
Do you have a pet?		
Do you find it easier to give orders than to take them?		
Do you consider yourself a highly competitive person?		
Do you find it easy to work with others?		
Do you laugh a lot?		
Do you take risks very often?		
Do you like to take risks?		
Do you think of the past a lot?		

	Yes	No
Do you think of the future a lot?		
Are you conscious of having avoided talking to anyone here today?		
Are you conscious of having tried to fool anyone here today?		
Do you have strong guilt feelings?		
Do you have strong feelings of hostility?		
Do you express feelings easily?		
Do you feel that this is the best time in your life?		
Are you employed?		
Do you like the type of work you are doing (your profession, your occupation)?		
Do you find your present job fulfilling?		
Have you ever been involved in experience-based learning before this?		
Do you feel pressured to be here?		
Are you now or have you recently been in therapy?		
Do you have a peer working relationship with a woman?		
Do you have a peer working relationship with a man?		
Are you active in the women's movement?		
Do or did your parents have a happy marriage?		
Do you like your name?		
Have you ever felt discriminated against because of your sex?		
Have you ever felt discriminated against because of your age?		
Have you ever felt discriminated against because of your race or ethnic background?		
Do you or did you want your first child to be a boy?		
Do you or did you want your first child to be a girl?		
Have you been in your present job for a year?		
Have you been in your present job for three years?		

	Yes	No
Have you been in your present job for more than three years?		
Have you been given added responsibility in your present job since you took it?		
Do you feel that your pay in your present position is fair?		
Do you enjoy a good working relationship with your boss?		
Do you enjoy a good working relationship with your subordinates?		
Do you enjoy a good working relationship with your peers?		
Do you regularly do most of the housecleaning?		
Would you rather be somewhere else at the moment?		
Are you self-conscious driving with a passenger of the opposite sex?		
Are you self-conscious riding with a driver of the opposite sex?		
Do you get useful feedback on your work performance from your boss?		
Do you accept negative feedback easily?		
Are you comfortable in giving negative feedback to others?		
Do you feel secure in your job?		
Do you find that there are serious obstacles to your effectiveness in your work?		
Do you find that you have the authority to carry out your responsibilities?		
Do you find your work interesting?		
Do you find that your work gives you enough opportunity for personal and professional growth?		
Do you feel that there is room for advancement in your work?		
Do you feel that you are achieving something significant in your work?		

	Yes	No

Do you want a new position within the next year? ____|____

Do you place a lot of importance on clothes? ____|____

Do you like to try eating new foods? ____|____

Would you really like to live in another part of the world? ____|____

Do you have a serious health problem? ____|____

Do you feel that you are working to your full capacity? ____|____

Are you interested in further formal education? ____|____

Are you artistic? ____|____

Are you mechanically inclined? ____|____

Do you get a lot of fun out of life? ____|____

Do you have any productive activity outside of work? ____|____

Do you enjoy competitive sports? ____|____

Do you believe in a divine power? ____|____

2. When you have finished answering the questions, choose the 10 you would most like to ask your group and ask them. As each question is asked, indicate to your group what your position is by a hand signal: raise your hand to say "yes," put your thumb down to say "no," fold your arms to pass. Be sure to answer the questions you ask. (*10 minutes*)

Passing means that you do not want to indicate your position at this time. It is OK to pass. You do not have to defend yourself for passing, but if you do, try to understand your reasons for doing so. We encourage you not to choose passing merely because you are uncertain or confused about a question.

We ask you here to indicate, simply and quickly, your choices and experiences concerning each question. You are also asked to observe as well as you can the choices of the others who are sharing this experience with you. However, you are asked not to discuss or explain your choices yet. Merely sharing your answers to these questions nonverbally with your group will produce a large amount of data in a short period of time with no need to explain, justify, or explore the differences. There will be time for discussion later.

Move through your questions quickly, but slowly enough to register where others are on each question. If all members of your group cannot see each other, rearrange the seating in the room to correct this condition. It is important for everyone to be able to look around and see how others in the group "vote," particularly if the group is large and data are needed to help members choose their subgroups. The questions are designed to make this possible.

When you have finished choosing from the list in the workbook, propose any additional questions of your own which you think would be of interest or use to you and your group. Be sure to leave some time for this.

3. Groups too large to function as one group will now form subgroups of four to five people. (*10 minutes*) Small groups can skip this step and go on to Step 4.

Maintaining the same subgroup throughout Life Work Planning deepens perceptions and broadens the base for feedback. A change in the groups, while it does allow experience with a greater number of participants, often limits the depth of your learning and sharing.

Take time now for a period of verbal negotiation to choose groups. Start with what you already know about each other from the past, from your informal conversation, and from the activities of the workshop so far. Use the negotiation period to check out impressions and hunches, ask questions, and find out what you need to know to make a relatively informed choice.

If you feel that you do not know people well enough to choose, do the best you can with the data you have. People generally make surprisingly logical choices in these circumstances.

It is important to realize that you are responsible for the choice you make. You will be spending a good deal of time (but not all of the time) with your subgroup and will be sharing a great deal back and forth with them. It is important to select people with whom you feel you can work comfortably and effectively.

4. This next set of questions continues our focus on key issues in life and work. We ask you to share with members of your subgroup some highlights of your experience and some perceptions which will let them begin to know *who you are. We* propose the questions— only *you* know the answers!

Take turns now sharing with your group answers to the questions listed below. All members of your group should have the opportunity to answer each question before you go on to the next one. You will have to work quickly. Set your timer at the required time for each question so that no one will have to watch a clock. It will be the responsibility of your group to make sure everyone gets a fair share of time.

There are no expected or wrong answers to these questions. People will respond differently because people are different. The point is to explore some of these differences and, from them, learn something about yourself and others. You have three minutes for each question except for questions *g* and *j*. (*30 minutes*)

a. What was your high point of the last week? Talk about it briefly.

b. Who is the one person who has done the most to make you who you are? How was that person significant for you?

c. What was the most risky decision you ever made in your life? Why was the risk so great?

d. Tell about one missed opportunity in your life.

e. What is the one thing about yourself you like the best?

f. If, by magic, you could change one thing about yourself, what would it be? Why?

g. One-minute questions that can be answered with a word or phrase:
   (1) What is the one skill you value the most?
   (2) What did you always want to be when you were young?
   (3) Who is your favorite hero? Why?
   (4) Where do you expect to be living 30 years from now?

h. Suppose you were told that you have six months to live. What would you do in that time?

i. To whom in the group do you feel closest? Why?

j. You have one minute to say anything you want to your subgroup — without using any words.

5. When you have finished with the sharing questions, take a few minutes to explore with your group your reactions to the introductory activities. What have you learned and felt? Talk about the trust level in your group. If you are not comfortable with the trust level in your group, what can you do about it? (*10 minutes*)

On the following pages is a briefing on constructive openness, which deals with how trust grows. You may wish to read it at this time. Questions at the end of the briefing focus on the experience you are having with your group.

Constructive openness

In the introductory activities, you have been more or less open with others and others have been more or less open with you.

What is it to be an open person, to have an open relationship, to behave openly? Joe Luft and Harry Ingham have developed the Johari Window to describe personal and interpersonal openness.

THE JOHARI WINDOW

	Known to self	Not known to self
Known to others	Open	Blind
Not known to others	Hidden	Unknown

The window represents your whole person.

The part of you that is known to yourself as well as others is called the *open* area. The open area is that part of you—your perceptions, feelings, and needs—which you freely share with others by your behavior (your words and actions). It is your comfort zone.

The part that is known to yourself but not to others is called the *hidden* area. The hidden area represents perceptions, feelings, and needs that you have not yet revealed to others through your behavior. You share your hidden area by opening up your behavior, by self-disclosure.

The part that is known to others but not to yourself is called the *blind* area. The blind area involves behavior, perceptions, feelings, and needs that you are not aware of although other people are. You find out about your blind area through feedback from others—that is, *if* you are willing and able to hear it. ("Would that God the gift would give us, to see ourselves as others see us.")

The part that is known neither to yourself nor to others is called the *unknown* area. The unknown area is that part of your behavior, perceptions, feelings, and needs which you have not yet discovered or which you once knew and have forgotten. Experiment and play help you to probe into your unknown area. Small children are experts at self-discovery simply because they are experts at play. As we grow older, we tend to lose our capacity to play, test, experiment, and fool around. If the unknown has been suppressed or repressed, therapy may be needed to help bring it to light. Life Work Planning is not designed to be therapy.

You can use the Johari Window to look at yourself and to help you to understand how open you are and what growth in openness means to you. You can also use it to look at the relationships in which you are involved—one to one, one to group, and group to group.

Assume that the window describes the relationship between you and someone else in the group with whom you are now working. The four quadrants· represent the total relationship. The quadrant of the window that describes what you and another actually share in your relationship is the open area. In an established or intimate relationship, your behavior tends to give free, easy access to the real you. Your open area is very large. In a new or more casual relationship, you may limit yourself to role behavior or to behavior which is guarded or socially conventional, thereby sharing yourself selectively. Your open area may be very small. As you get to know and trust another, and as your behavior and what you reveal of yourself by it become more open, the open area grows in size. Your relationship develops and grows beyond what it was when you both move into the blind, the hidden, and the unknown— as you become more open within yourselves and toward each other. The broken line in the diagram represents potential growth in openness, the growth of your open area.

Or assume that the window describes yourself. You are probably more open in some places, at some times, and with some people than otherwise. There are probably certain issues, feelings, or experiences about which you find it easier to be open than about others. You will find it more difficult to hear about some behaviors and perceptions than others without being defensive. There are probably some parts of yourself of which you are simply unaware or which frighten or excite you when you encounter them.

Enlarging your area of openness by reducing the hidden, the blind, and the unknown is always a little risky. There is risk to you and risk to the other. Will you hurt someone? Will you make someone angry? Will someone reject you? What will people think about you? What will you find out about yourself? The risks, the pain, and the fear of being open can be strong deterrents. When is openness worthwhile? When is it possible? When is it constructive? A question not so often asked is: "What is the risk of *not* being open?"

Developing openness involves risk and assumes a certain degree of trust. There is a paradox here—people tend to take less risk where there is less trust, yet it takes risk to develop trust.

The norm we have found most productive in this program is to respect the limitations you and others choose to place on openness and to leave you free to go at your own pace and to your own depth. If you do choose to limit your openness, we think it is important for you to be clear to yourself why you are making this choice.

For most people, openness is not an absolute value. It is not always possible or even desirable. Most people need a good reason for being open—a purpose beyond openness itself. For instance, you may be open because you care enough about improving a relationship to make it worth the effort. If a certain measure of caring does not come across in your attempt to be open, you may well be perceived as meddling, intrusive, coercive, manipulative, threatening, aggressive, or even hostile.

If, in the name of openness, you are not sensitive and responsive to others, you may wind up serving only your own needs and ignoring the needs of others. Openness is sharing; it is a contradiction to thrust it on others. Others have to be willing to be open with you. Otherwise openness becomes coercive.

Confronting another openly may not be nearly as risky as accepting the confrontation of another and responding to it. For example, when you take a risk and initiate openness with me, I may be running an even greater risk by being open in return. I have many safer options: to evade, to flee, to be defensive, to attack, to be silent. When you offer your openness, I can back off. When I accept your openness, we are both committed.

Defenses are not all bad. We all need them and use them from time to time. Openness should never be an excuse for stripping others of their defenses. Openness should build trust to the point where others feel safe enough to be able to drop their defenses of their own accord.

The aim of openness is not to change, help, or convince others but to deepen your relationship by sharing an understanding of each other's perceptions, feeling, and needs. While this shared awareness leaves each person responsible for his or her own behavior, it also opens up new behavioral alternatives. Faced with the perceptions, feelings, and needs of another about whom I care, I may well choose to alter my behavior. The choice among alternatives, the change that grows out of openness, remains self-determined.

It should be evident by now that being open is not the same as being personal. Revealing a lot of personal details about your past can be a defensive substitute for dealing with here-and-now behavior, perceptions, feelings, and needs.

Openness sometimes reveals conflict. Conflict is OK. You have rights and needs. So do others. Sometimes they collide. Conflict must be resolved if relationships are to grow.

Power as a basis of resolving conflict—although it has some short-term advantages—is ultimately counterproductive and destructive of relationships. It tends to produce win-lose solutions.

Trust and shared acceptance of different perceptions, needs, and feelings on both sides as a basis of resolving conflicts tends to produce win-win solutions. These are consistently better solutions and contribute to the growth of relationships. Removing power from conflict resolution tends to stimulate creativity and commitment in developing and implementing solutions to problems.

You might find the following questions useful for reflection and for sharing:

How open have you been with others in your group?

How open do you feel others have been with you?

When were you aware of disclosing your hidden area?

Are there parts of your hidden area you do not feel comfortable about disclosing?

Have you received any feedback that gave you insight into your blind area?

Did any of the questions lead you to explore your unknown area?

How comfortable do you feel as you think of sharing Life Work Planning with your group?

Your life line

WHERE HAVE YOU BEEN?

90 minutes

While Life Work Planning does not urge you to dwell on the past, a quick but insightful look at the past can provide a perspective from which you can look ahead.

We all give some thought to our past experience — sometimes we feel overwhelmed by the joy of a good life to date, sometimes we find ourselves fighting to overcome poor judgments and ill fortune. Whatever our past experience, we can learn from it. We suggest that you take this comprehensive look at your life to date, learning what you can to think through your life ahead more productively.

We have found the Life Line a very effective means for doing this. The new experience of visualizing your whole life-span — past, present and future — in colors and symbols frees creative energy for a new perspective and new insights.

Within your group, this overview provides information for introducing you to each other in some depth. In a way, it also introduces you to yourself. It highlights what from your past is operating on the present. It provides a context for what you will learn about yourself in later activities.

In the Life Line activity, we ask you to draw. Many of us feel awkward and ill-equipped when asked to draw anything. You may even stumble on sources of this insecurity as the activity takes you back into your childhood. Try to let yourself become involved in this new form of expression — if it *is* new. As in other activities in Life Work Planning, the more you let yourself go, the more fun you will have and the more you will learn about yourself. Don't panic. Anybody can draw a line. Drawing ability has nothing to do with the task. You may be surprised at your own creativity once you get into the activity.

Experiment with symbols, colors, cartoons. You might even write in signs and labels if you wish, but do minimize writing. In many of the following activities, you will be called upon to write about yourself; the point here is to get away from words and to try to learn about yourself in a new way. Experiment and play a little and see what happens.

For this activity you will need a large sheet of paper (newsprint, easel paper, a large paper bag cut up, etc.) and a quantity of felt pens or crayons in at least four colors. Felt pens are more expensive than crayons, but they produce more vivid colors. People can easily work from a common supply.

Following, there is a double page in the Workbook for drawing your life line, but you will find this a much more challenging and productive activity if you use really large sheets of paper and a wide selection of drawing materials.

1. On the large sheet of paper, draw a single line that represents your life — its course to date and where the future may take it. Your line may take any direction and any shape. Identify the beginning of your life line with your birth date. Identify the end with the date you select as likely for your death. Then place an X on the line to show the spot that represents where you are today. (*5 minutes*) **Please finish this step before going on to the next.**

2. Take some time now to fill in some details on your life line in order to create a comprehensive picture of what your life has been and what it might look like in the future.

Let's begin with your history. Knowing where and what you come from will help you in your future plans and decisions. We'd like you to represent in some way on your line those details from your past life which seem to you to be significant. These details may be important experiences, feelings, relationships, stages, events—whatever from your past life still influences the present. (*25 minutes*)

You *may* find it useful to use the questions below to jog your memory and to help you remember significant details. Do not be limited by this and do not get so involved in the questions that you limit your time in the drawing. Let yourself go. Play with color and form. Try to express your *feelings* about details of the past and the impact each had on you.

Who have been the most influential people in your   Dates
life, and in what ways have they been influential?

_____   _____

_____   _____

_____   _____

_____   _____

_____   _____

What were the major interests in your early life?

_____   _____

_____   _____

_____   _____

_____   _____

_____   _____

What were the most critical things that have happened, that made you who you are? They may be positive or negative.

Dates

_____ _____

_____ _____

_____ _____

_____ _____

_____ _____

_____ _____

What were the most important high points and low points in your life?

_____ _____

_____ _____

_____ _____

_____ _____

_____ _____

What have been the significant work experiences you have had?

_____ _____

_____ _____

_____ _____

_____ _____

_____ _____

What have been the significant decisions of your
life?   Dates

_____   _____

_____   _____

_____   _____

_____   _____

_____   _____

_____   _____

What other things occur to you to put on your life
line?

_____   _____

_____   _____

_____   _____

_____   _____

_____   _____

_____   _____

3.   You may now want to project into the future a little and sketch out
     what you would like the rest of your life line to look and feel like.

4.   When you have completed drawing your life line, share your draw-
     ing in your group. Explain it as needed. Share your thoughts and
     feelings about it. Be sure to listen to the questions and perceptions
     of others after they look at your sketch. Your group may even want
     to hang everyone's life lines on the wall for comparison and future
     reference. (*10 to 15 minutes per person*)

The following questions for reflection and/or sharing may stimulate discussion.

What is your first reaction to this activity? Thoughts? Feelings?

Where have you made significant decisions about your work, life, or both? Where have you let yourself drift along?

Are the important things on your life line connected with your work, your life, or both? What does this say to you?

What patterns or trends are there in your past experience?

Did you consider other persons in your life line? How have these persons affected you?

Is there any significance in your most recent experiences? If so, where are they taking you?

What colors, symbols, and shapes have you used? How are they significant?

How do you feel now about your past life experiences? About the "you" who lived them?

Skills
of openness

Being open has to do with behavior (words and actions—what you say and do) and the perceptions, feelings, and needs which behavior conveys (what you see, hear, feel, and need). Perceptions may be of facts, behaviors, statements, or thoughts. Needs may include what you want, wish, ask for, or demand.

You can be open in two senses. You can be open to sharing yourself with others or to accepting what others share with you.

When your behavior conveys your perceptions, feelings, and needs directly and freely, you are being open. You are opening yourself to others in order to share yourself.

When you receive the perceptions, feelings, and needs which others intend to convey in their behavior and accept them as facts, you are being open. You are opening yourself to others to receive and accept them. Acceptance does not necessarily mean agreement. You can accept a difference as a fact and, for the moment, suspend judgment about it. Although acceptance means receiving without judgment, it does not mean receiving without reaction or feeling.

Below is a collection of specific communication skills which tend to build open and trusting relationships. Your communication will tend to be more open if you try to:

˙. . . Separate out thoughts from feelings:
"I think that is a good idea, but I feel very threatened by it."

. . . Separate out behavior from feelings:
"When you just said that (your behavior), I felt very angry (my feeling reaction)."

When you are this specific about which behavior of mine you are reacting to and what your reaction is, you give me a chance to deal with you, myself, or both of us. It is an opening, freeing response, which gives me good, clear information about you and about me. It invites us both to examine and understand our interaction.

. . . Describe a person's behavior rather than being evaluative or judgmental:
Judgmental: "You're so rude!"
Descriptive: "I hadn't finished yet, and you began to speak."

. . . Be specific rather than general:
General: "You never watch where you're going!"
Specific: "You bumped my arm."

. . . Avoid the word "that" in making a feeling statement:
"I feel that you were wrong." (*Judgment*)
"I feel that this kind of statement is unpatriotic." (*Opinion*)
"I feel angry." (*Feeling*)

. . . Take responsibility for your feelings and needs, owning them as yours:
Avoiding responsibility: "You make me mad."
Taking responsibility: "I feel angry."
Avoiding responsibility: "When people fail, they feel defeated."
"Everyone feels defeated when he or she fails."
"When we fail, we feel defeated."
"When you fail, you feel defeated."
Taking responsibility: "When I fail, I feel defeated."

. . . Let the other draw his or her own conclusions:
Leading question: "You'll always be mother's little helper won't you?" (This lays a heavy burden on the child.)
Open statement: "The yard looks good and I feel very pleased."
(This leaves the child free to feel as good as he or she is able to.)

. . . Be direct in describing your feelings, rather than indirect in expressing them.

There are many ways of expressing feelings indirectly. These can be very confusing to others, because they focus on something else (usually on the other person) and tend to hide what you are really saying. Most indirect statements are "you" statements which can, with care, be translated into more direct "I" statements.

The following are some common examples of indirect expressions of feelings—and possible translations:

Generalization: "You're always picking on me!" ("I feel threatened by you.")

Name calling: "You dope!" ("I am angry with you.")

Accusation: "You enjoy putting people down." ("When you just said that, I felt hurt.")

Judgment: Praise—"You're great!" ("I really like you.") Blame—"You're stupid!" ("I don't like what you just did.")

Question: "Is it safe to drive so fast?" ("I'm afraid of going this fast. Please slow down!")

Sarcasm: "Who needs friends like you?" ("What you just did was not helpful.")

Command: "Shut up!" ("I'm so angry I can't think.")

Giving solutions: "Why don't you go and play with your sister?" ("I really want to get this work done, and I'm worried about it.")

Teaching, warning, advising: "Don't ever force a tool." ("I'm afraid you'll hurt yourself doing it that way.")

Silence: (Which can mean anything.)

. . . Avoid "why" questions. Such questions seem to imply judgment or criticism and invite defense or justification rather than further exploration of behavior:

"Why" question: "Why did you say that?"

Direct statement: "I wish you would clarify for me what you just said," or, "I don't understand what you just said."

. . . State the other's perception, feeling, or need in your own words to check out whether you have understood properly.

This is called *paraphrasing,* or *active listening.* Be sure to paraphrase the sender's perceptions, feelings, and needs rather than just parrot the sender's words or actions.

. . . Be provisional rather than absolute. Check to see if your perception is correct:

Absolute: "Boy, are you mad!"

Provisional and checking out: "You seem to be reacting strongly. Are you angry?"

Being provisional will often let you check out your perceptions of the other. Simply state without judgment what you perceive the other to be perceiving, feeling, or needing and ask if this is accurate. This is important, because behavior often masks real perceptions, feelings, or needs.

. . . Avoid responses that turn off, tune out, put down, ignore, or deal past what someone says by doing the following:

Moralizing: "You shouldn't feel that way."

Giving advice: "Why don't you learn how to get along with people better?"
Interpreting: "I'll bet you don't really mean that."
Questioning: "How long has this been going on?"
Reassuring: "You'll be OK, don't worry."
Avoiding: "Let's talk about something more pleasant."

An excellent and more complete discussion of making "I" statements and active listening or paraphrasing — with many vivid examples — is found in Chapters 3 and 6 of *Parent Effectiveness Training.**

---

* Thomas Gordon, *Parent Effectiveness Training,* A Plume Book, New American Library, New York, 1975.

Peak work experience

WHEN ARE YOU "ALL THERE"?   75 minutes

[*Since*] . . . *people in peak experiences are* most *their identities, closest to their real selves, most idiosyncratic, it would seem that this is an especially important source of clean and uncontaminated data* [*about themselves*]; *i.e., invention is reduced to a minimum, and discovery increased to a maximum.* . . .

The person in the peak experience feels more integrated (unified, whole, all-of-a-piece), than at other times. He also looks (to the observer) more integrated in various ways . . . e.g., less split or dissociated, less fighting against himself, more at peace with himself, less split between an experiencing self and an observing self, more one-pointed, more harmoniously organized, more efficiently organized with all his parts functioning very nicely with each other, more synergic, with less internal friction, etc. . . .

The person in the peak experiences usually feels himself to be at the peak of his powers, using all his capacities at the best and fullest. In Rogers's nice phrase, he feels "fully functioning." He feels more intelligent, more perceptive, wittier, stronger, or more graceful than at other times. He is at his best, at concert pitch, at the top of his form. This is not only felt subjectively but can be seen by the observer. He is no longer wasting effort fighting and restraining himself; muscles are no longer fighting muscles. In the normal situation, part of our capacities are used for action, and part are wasted on restraining these same capacities. Now there is no waste; the totality of the capacities can be used for action. He becomes like a river without dams. . . .

A slightly different aspect of fully functioning is effortlessness and ease of functioning when one is at one's best. . . .

The person in peak experiences feels himself, more than at other times, to be the responsible, active, creating center of his activities and of his perceptions. . . .

He is now most free of blocks, inhibitions, cautions, fears, doubts, controls, reservations, self-criticisms, brakes. . . .

He is therefore more spontaneous, more expressive, more innocently behaving . . . , more natural . . . , more uncontrolled and freely flowing outward. . . .

In the peak experiences, the individual is most here-now, most free of the past and of the future in various senses, most "all there" in the experience. . . .*

—Abraham H. Maslow

Few of us can recall a peak experience in our working lives which lifted us *all the way* to the heights described by Maslow. We can scan our own experience to find those moments which moved us toward that height.

A look at a peak experience in your past work or study provides a very stimulating and productive look at yourself. Allowing yourself to

---

* Abraham H. Maslow, *Toward a Psychology of Being,* Van Nostrand, Princeton, N.J., 1962, pp. 98–102.

reexperience a peak is to get in touch with your deepest self. This offers you information that will be very useful as you move on to planning a life more and more filled with peak experiences, coming ever closer to Maslow's description.

The method here is to relive in vivid detail a past work experience which most called on your talents, heightened your energies, stimulated your very being, gave you real satisfaction and fulfillment. You will then reflect on this experience to see what made it special for you.

1. Take three minutes to compose yourself, breathe deeply, and relax. **Slow down.**

2. Now think back into the past and select out from your work experience one single episode that stands out as a peak experience. A peak experience is one that turned you on; gave you intense fulfillment, stimulation, satisfaction; made you feel good about yourself and the world; broke through the pattern of everyday life. In other words, a real high point. Select a specific event rather than a period of time. Focus on the work itself rather than on the moment of reward that might have followed from the work. (*7 minutes*)

    If you have some trouble identifying a peak work experience, remember that a peak experience does not have to be all that dramatic, public, spectacular, or newsworthy. What is important is that it was something that you found really satisfying. You are looking for a spark, a starter, something to build on.

    If you have little work experience, scan your school years, part-time jobs, hobbies, and interests. You might, in addition, look at work in your home, volunteer work, times when you helped people out, or brief work experiences from the past.

> *I can remember, for instance, working for a local ward heeler at election time when I was 8 to 12 years old. He was a beautiful man. I ran errands and knocked on doors. I can still feel my sense of importance, of being needed — of responsibility, involvement, and close, active association with a person who was a hero to me. To this day I cannot walk through the autumn leaves on a street without feeling the warmth and excitement of those times.*
>
> *AGK*

Now let yourself into *your* experience. Think about it, visualize it, try to relive it in every vivid detail. Where are you? What is the date and time? What led you to this moment? What are you doing? What skills and talents are you using? Who else is there? How do you feel? What are the results of what you are doing? Are there any other circumstances you can remember? Don't be afraid to feel good or proud — to enjoy your abilities. No censoring.

3. There are two steps in this portion of the activity. You will find it more productive for each person to complete both steps before you move on to the next member of the group. (*10 to 15 minutes per person*)

First, narrate the details of your peak work experience in the first person present as if it were going on here and now ("Today I am. . . ." instead of "Three years ago I was. . . ."). This helps you to catch the quality of your peak experience as if it were fresh and real. Get into it and live it as if you were doing it for the first time. Others in your group will help you speak in the first person present.

Second, when you finish relating your account, have your group help you identify the characteristics that made your peak experience different from other less stimulating, less exhilarating experiences. What did you value in this experience? Why did things go so well? What motivated you, turned you on, satisfied you, fulfilled you? List them below.

What made your experience a peak experience?

_____

_____

_____

_____

_____

_____

_____

_____

_____

_____

_____

_____

_____

4. When you and your group have finished sharing the work experience and making your lists, reflect on them and explore their significance with your group. The following questions may serve as a guide. (*10 minutes*)

How many items on your list do you experience in your present work situation?

Which items *could* you experience more fully in your current work? How?

Can you think now of other work situations in which these characteristics might be more available?

How do you feel about your list?

What have you learned about yourself?

Hygiene-motivation theory

The lists produced by groups working on the peak work experience have confirmed with amazing consistency Frederick Herzberg's widely known hygiene-motivation theory.* His findings may present a stimulating perspective for you.

Herzberg asked thousands of people at every level of many organizations what it was that satisfied them and gave them real fulfillment in a job situation and what it was that dissatisfied them and made them unhappy. As the table on the next page illustrates, he found that people generally listed a different set of factors for each question.

What dissatisfies people are factors in the work environment, like company policy and administration, salary, relationship with supervisor, work conditions, etc. If these are not up to standard, people will be dissatisfied.

Factors affecting job attitudes, as reported in 12 investigations

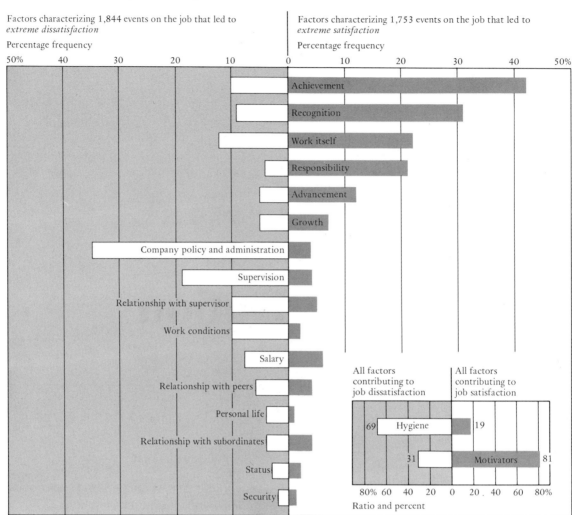

Factors characterizing 1,844 events on the job that led to *extreme dissatisfaction*

Percentage frequency

Factors characterizing 1,753 events on the job that led to *extreme satisfaction*

Percentage frequency

What satisfies people in a work situation are factors relating directly to the work itself, like the intrinsic interest of the work, the responsibility the work gives, recognition for the work, the sense of achievement in the work, the advancement the work affords, and the personal and professional growth gained through work. If these are present, people tend to find true satisfaction in their work.

Herzberg makes an interesting observation which stems from this difference. Satisfaction and dissatisfaction are not opposites. The opposite of being satisfied is not being dissatisfied; it is being *not satisfied.* Similarly, the opposite of being dissatisfied is not being satisfied, it is being *not dissatisfied.*

Herzberg calls dissatisfiers hygiene factors, like public health measures (sewage disposal, water purification) which do not make people healthy but keep them from getting sick. Attention to hygiene factors on the job keeps people from being dissatisfied but does not satisfy or motivate them. Dissatisfiers also tend to return to zero, like my hunger today, in spite of the fact that I ate well yesterday. Similarly, an increase in salary will stop dissatisfaction for a time, but soon it will turn up again. Real satisfiers or motivators tend to be more permanent.

The implication for Life Work Planning is that to enrich a job situation or to seek a job situation which is more enriching than the present one, you must look not only for ways to build against dissatisfaction but, more important, seek ways to build in satisfaction. Finding out about dissatisfiers is relatively easy. Pursuing real satisfaction may require sharper questioning.

Questions for a prospective employer or for your supervisor might include the following:

"How do you define responsibility?" "What are the controls placed upon my authority?" "To whom will I be accountable?" "For what?" Don't settle for generalities.

"Is it possible to perform complete units of work?"

"What specific authority will I have? Responsibility?"

"Will feedback on the quality of my work be given directly to me rather than through a supervisor?"

"When I feel willing and able, will I be able to take on new and more difficult tasks?"

"When will I be considered for a promotion? What will be the criteria for moving on to new responsibilities?"

"Will there be an opportunity for specialization, for developing expertise in any one area?"

"Will it be possible to train someone else to do my work, providing a replacement when I am given the opportunity to move on?"

"What evidence is there that I will be given increased accountability for my own work when I am ready for it?"

Making choices

AN EXERCISE

15 minutes

The Road Not Taken

Two roads diverged in a yellow wood,
And sorry I could not travel both
And be one traveler, long I stood
And looked down one as far as I could
To where it bent in the undergrowth;

Then took the other, as just as fair,
And having perhaps the better claim,
Because it was grassy and wanted wear;
Though as for that, the passing there
Had worn them really about the same,

And both that morning equally lay
In leaves no step had trodden black.
Oh, I kept the first for another day!
Yet knowing how way leads on to way,
I doubted if I should ever come back.

I shall be telling this with a sigh
Somewhere ages and ages hence:
Two roads diverged in a wood, and I—
I took the one less traveled by,
And that has made all the difference.*

—*Robert Frost*

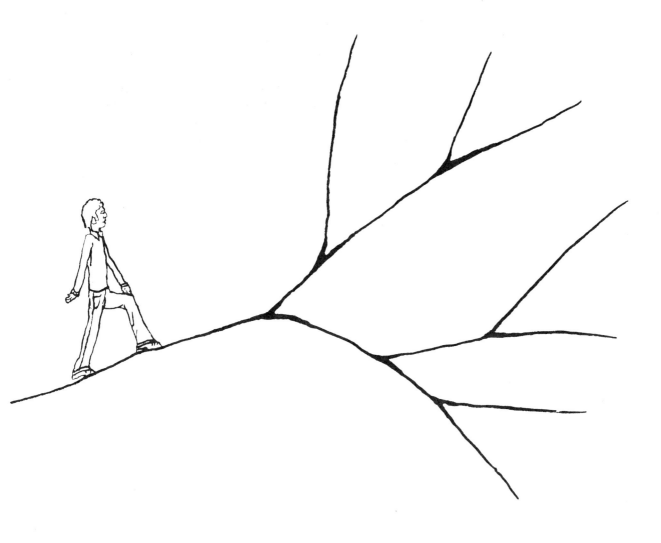

"I took the one . . . , and that has made all the difference." Our choices make our lives what they are. They do make a difference. Without choice, our life is programmed, determined, and out of our control. We merely succumb. Or we rebel.

At times, for many of us, to succumb seems far simpler than to choose. Perhaps it is not so strange, given its significance in our lives, that choice presents such a human dilemma. Faced with major choices, many of us become immobilized or at least tense. Our fears are many:

that we will make the wrong choice; that in making one choice, we rule out the other or the others; that we are unable to be fully committed to any one choice at all; that we can never change our minds; that being "locked in" to the choice we make today will "lock us in" to the person we are today or to the present circumstances. The excitement of choosing a school, a job, a house, a field of study, or a spouse is often clouded—and often put off—by our fear of "taking the one."

One answer, of course, is to avoid making any choice at all and to drift with circumstance or with the choice of others. But as Harvey Cox says so well in his much quoted phrase, "Not to decide is to decide." He confronts us with the reality that to choose to drift is a choice we can make. Is that the one you want to make?

Our belief, and certainly a basic rationale for this program, is that we can make choices that accurately reflect who we are—our values, interests, experience, capacities. We must increase our ability to identify our priorities and to make those choices that can bring us real satisfaction, joy, love, and productivity.

This activity is an exercise in choice. We offer you the following five alternatives and ask you to rank them, by putting the worst *first*. The ranking is not meant to be easy; it may give you some insight into your choice-making process and into the feelings you have about making choices.*

1. Rank the following "heroes" in descending order of preference (worst first) and decide why you have chosen this order. (*5 minutes*)

    a. The industrialist who, in public, gives lip service to antipollution concerns but orders his factory to emit heavy pollutants at night when they cannot be detected.

    b. The man who dislikes swimming with blacks so much that he forms a swimming club with the unwritten but clear understanding that no blacks will be admitted.

    c. The father who, when he finds his 2-year-old son playing with his genitals, slaps him across the face and says, "Don't you know that will make you go crazy?"

    d. The college student who sells pot to high school students at cost because he sincerely thinks they should have a chance to experience it.

    e. The man who works for a firm developing chemical warfare agents and who, when confronted by his college-age son about how he can go on doing it, snaps back: "Shut up! The money I make there is putting you through college!"

---

* This activity was used in a workshop conducted by Dr. Sidney B. Simon in Putney, Vt., in May 1970.

Ranked Items

1.

2.

3.

4.

5.

2. Talk about this activity with your group using the following questions for reflection, sharing, or both. (*10 minutes*)

What are the varieties in values and preferences among you?

What were your feelings about having to make a choice?

What differing assumptions did each of you make about each item?

How does this experience relate to your general approach to making choices?

If you have the time and interest, you might try these additional sets of choices using the same directions and questions.

Rank the following, putting first the one you would least like to have happen to you (worst first . . .); then decide why you chose as you did.

a. Suffer a real loss of functional intelligence.

b. Suffer the loss of a hand.

c. Undergo a nervous breakdown.

d. Undergo complete loss of material goods by flood or fire with no insurance and no reserve.

e. Have your best friend turn on you completely.

Ranked Items

1.

2.

3.

4.

5.

Which risk would you least like to take, in descending order (worst first . . .), and why?

a. Bet $10,000 in a gamble.

b. Go into business for yourself.

c. Without a job assured, move to a remote place where you have always wanted to live.

d. Have an affair.

e. Risk arrest in a public demonstration for or against something you feel strongly about.

Ranked Items

1.

2.

3.

4.

5.

The fantasy work situation

WHAT CAN YOU DO?

About 95 percent of us utilize only about 5 percent of our potential. Many behavioral scientists—including Gordon Allport, Abraham Maslow, Gardner Murphy, Carl Rogers, Margaret Mead, Herb Otto, and others—subscribe to this confronting hypothesis. When we look at the achievements of champions, heroes, the great, the noble, the self-actualizing, or people under stress or pressure, we are astonished at what they can do. Something in us recognizes our greater potential and knows that we can tap it more often than we do.

Surprisingly, many of us are more comfortable and familiar with our weaknesses and limitations than we are with our strengths. Some feel that pride and boasting are wrong, and that whatever we have is not really ours anyway. Some of us might feel guilty or defensive about not having done more with our abilities than we have. Some of us have a tendency to talk ourselves down and minimize our positive sides. In the terms of transactional analysis, we who still feel not OK may have difficulty concentrating much on what is OK about ourselves.

What can you do? That's a hard question for most of us to answer. Vague generalities are simple—"I can't do anything well," "I can do anything I want to do," "I really don't do anything perfectly."

It is fairly obvious that you can't plan ahead, think ahead, and make choices for yourself if you are not in touch with your real capacities and capabilities. There is much that you have done in your lifetime, no matter how short, that you might now choose to put to use. You will not want to use *all* these skills in the days ahead, but it is well to take a survey of them in order to identify those you would like to use in the future.

This is another activity in Life Work Planning in which the more you let yourself go—the more you brainstorm and freewheel—the more you will learn about yourself.

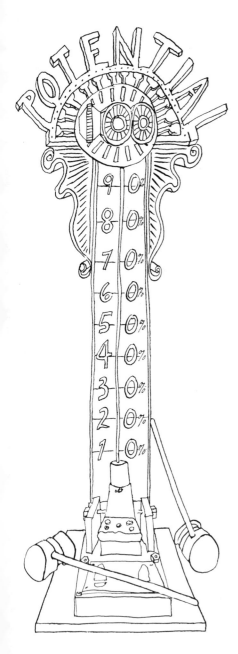

1. On the work sheets below, make an exhaustive list of all the things you can do. (*10 to 15 minutes*)

Consider the broadest possible range of personal skills, talents, abilities, strengths, resources, capabilities, potentials, things you can do. In addition to things you can do now, go back over the years to things you used to do—to camp days, summer jobs, school, house or garden work, hobbies, life skills. Include potentials you can develop. Put aside fears of being boastful, proud, egocentric. Brainstorm. Blue-sky. Let one item suggest another. Do not censor. Put down everything that comes to mind even if it seems silly or insignificant (thread a needle or ride a bike), or if you think you can do it but are not quite sure (write a novel, get a law degree), or even if you do not like to do it (clean a house, clean a fish). Include things which are physical, mental, spiritual, relational, feelings, fun, serious, professional. There are no wrong answers. One person had only two things on his list because they were the only things he could do perfectly. Try to move beyond this!

2. There are three steps in this portion of the activity. You will find it more productive for each person to complete all three before you move on to the next member of the group. (*10 to 15 minutes per person*)

First, meet with your group and share your list. Read your list slowly and reflectively so that others have time to absorb it.

Second, after you read your list, pause and listen without comment or protest as the group members suggest to you additional items they think you have overlooked. Add these items to your list **without censoring any.**

Third, fantasize the ideal occupation or work situation in which it would be possible to make **maximum use** of your skills. Build into your fantasy details such as location, relationships, circumstances, or working conditions. Build a dream out of what you can do. Don't worry about reality constraints. There are plenty of reality checks built into later activities in the program. You have the options of building a fantasy yourself and having your group react, having the group build it for you, or building it together with your group. If you have more than one dream, select the best or find a way to combine more than one. Let yourself go, have some fun, and see what happens. Be as specific and detailed as is useful.

SKILLS, TALENTS, ABILITIES, RESOURCES, STRENGTHS, CAPABILITIES, POTENTIALS, THINGS I CAN DO

_____   _____   _____

_____   _____   _____

_____   _____   _____

_____   _____   _____

_____   _____   _____

_____   _____   _____

_____   _____   _____

_____   _____   _____

_____   _____   _____

_____   _____   _____

_____   _____   _____

_____   _____   _____

_____   _____   _____

_____   _____   _____

_____   _____   _____

Feedback
skills

Giving and getting feedback plays a key role in being open. By enabling you to see the impact on another of what you say and do, feedback can illuminate your blind area. Feedback on your behavior, on how you come across, on how others see you versus how you see yourself, can also help you to consider some alternative ways of behaving. If feedback is not given constructively, it may just encourage defensiveness or simply be destructive.

Feedback will tend to be constructive if . . .

. . . It is asked for or at least welcome rather than imposed.

. . . It is well timed. Feedback is most often useful when it is given immediately after the behavior in question. Sometimes it is better to wait, especially if the recipient is angry, confused, upset, or defensive and not inclined to listen.

. . . It is spontaneous and direct.

. . . It is not saved up and dumped all at once. This is usually accompanied by a buildup of feeling which is hard to sort out from the message.

. . . It is checked by paraphrase to ensure accurate, clear communication.

. . . It is checked for validity against the perceptions of others.

. . . It sorts out perceptions, feelings, and needs.

. . . It meets the needs of the recipient as well as the needs of the one giving the feedback.

. . . It is specific rather than general. Examples of exact statements and behavior are useful.

. . . It leaves recipients free to do with it what they want, to change or not as they choose.

. . . It simply describes the recipient's behavior and its impact on others, without making any judgments about the person.

. . . It is given in a climate of trust, with a feeling of caring and support.

. . . It focuses on things recipients can do something about.

. . . Negative feedback is preceded by positive feedback. This helps give support.

. . . It is received nondefensively. A good rule of thumb is to ask only clarifying questions when receiving feedback and say little else.

. . . Recipients have a chance to say what they think and feel about the feedback when it is all over. This can lead to a better understanding of why people behave the way they do.

An inventory

WHAT WOULD YOU LIKE TO DO?   20 minutes

1. In the first column below, make a list of the 10 things you would most like to do before you die. (*5 minutes*) **Make your list before looking ahead to Step 2.**

1. _____   _____

2. _____   _____

3. _____   _____

4. _____   _____

5. _____   _____

6. _____   _____

7. _____   _____

8. _____   _____

9. _____   _____

10. _____   _____

2. When you have finished your list, indicate in the second column what you are doing or going to do to accomplish these things. (*5 minutes*)

3. Share with your group your reactions and feelings. You may find it useful to read your lists to each other. (*10 minutes*) Some suggested questions:

How many of your items are related to work? Life?

Did you see an opportunity for personal growth in some dimension?

Were there any surprises? Did you learn anything?

How many items involved relationships with others?

A self-inventory

75 minutes

Below the level of the problem situation about which the individual is complaining—behind the trouble with studies, or wife, or employer, or with his own uncontrollable or bizarre behavior, or with his frightening feelings, lies one central search. It seems to me that at bottom each person is asking, "Who am I, really? How can I get in touch with this real self, underlying all my surface behavior? How can I become myself?" *

—*Carl R. Rogers*

1. For this activity you will need 15 small sheets of paper. Write a series of 15 statements about yourself beginning with the words "I am . . . ." Put each "I am . . . ." on a new sheet. Brainstorm and do not censor; put down whatever comes to mind. (*10 to 15 minutes*) **Do not look ahead to Steps 2 and 3 until you have finished Step 1.**

---

* Carl R. Rogers, *On Becoming a Person,* Houghton Mifflin, Boston, 1961, p. 108.

51

You can list your 15 "I am . . . ." statements below on this page, but it tends to be more productive to use the separate sheets of paper.

_____

_____

_____

_____

_____

_____

_____

_____

_____

_____

_____

_____

_____

_____

2. Discard the five "I am . . . ." statements that are least important to you and arrange the remaining ten in the order of their importance to you. You might wish to number them in this order. (*5 minutes*)

3. Read your "I am . . . ." statements to your group and talk about them before moving on to the next person. (*10 minutes per person*)

   An optional procedure here is to exchange your "I am . . . ." statements with someone else in your group and have that person read them. When you hear them read by somebody else, you may gain a new perspective on what you wrote down. Below are some points to explore as you share your lists.

How many "I am . . . ." statements indicate roles you play (I am a mother, I am a teacher, I am a lawyer, etc.) and how many indicate personal characteristics (I am strong, I am intelligent, I am easy to anger, etc.)?

How many are statements about how you are seen by others (I am loved, I am appreciated, etc.) as opposed to how you see yourself (I am a loving person, I am appreciative, etc.)?

How many statements are work-oriented and how many are life-oriented? What does this mean to you?

How consistent are the data here with other data the group has about you?

How many statements are what you want people to hear or what you think other people expect to hear?

What surprised you in doing the list or looking at it?

Do your statements focus on the past, the future, or the present?

What surprises, new ideas, or feelings occur to you?

Preferences

WHAT DO YOU LIKE TO DO?

15 minutes

1. Make a list of the 10 things you most like to do. (*5 minutes*) **Make your list before looking ahead to Step 2.**

1. _____   _____

2. _____   _____

3. _____   _____

4. _____   _____

5. _____   _____

6. _____   _____

7. _____   _____

8. _____   _____

9. _____   _____

10. _____   _____

2. When you have finished your list, note the date when, as best you can remember, you last did each item on your list. (*1 minute*)

3. Now share with your group your reactions and feelings, surprises, things you have learned, and your questions. You may find it useful to read your lists to each other. (*9 minutes*) The following questions might be useful.

How many of the items on your list have you not done for a significant period of time?

How many of the items on your list are work-oriented and how many are life-oriented?

How many of the items on your list are things you do alone, and how many are things you do with other people?

How many had trouble listing 10 items? How many had trouble limiting the list to 10?

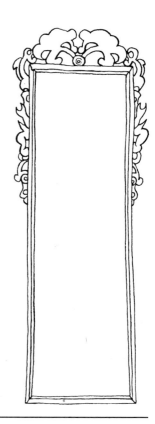

Two self-portraits

WHO ARE YOU?

Now we'd like you to take felt pens in hand again, this time to take another look at how you see and feel about yourself now.

Do you feel like a red circle or a blue square? What color are your feelings about your kitchen sink, your desk? What shape do others see in you? What color would you like to be? We are so used to *talking* about ourselves that the experience of representing ourselves and our feelings in color, shape, and symbols can provide exciting new insights.

For this activity you will need a large sheet of paper and a quantity of crayons or felt marking pens in at least four colors. Several people can easily work from a common supply. Although there is space in this workbook on the following two pages for your drawings, usually a really large sheet of paper permits greater freedom and variety of expression.

1. On the large sheet of paper, make two drawings of yourself using one of the following sets of themes. (*20 minutes*)

Myself at work and myself away from work.

The role(s) I play and who I am.

How I see myself and how others see me.

How I am and how I'd like to be.

Try to select a set of themes which gives you a challenge, one which provokes your interest. If a given set of themes touches on an area of personal confusion or conflict, that may be a good reason to select it.

Be as abstract or as concrete as you wish. Arrange your drawings on the paper in any way you wish. Do not limit yourself to a picture of the face. Freely experiment with symbols, images, colors, shapes, anything you can think of. Do try to get away from the verbal mode of expression.

Artistic achievement is not the objective. Plunge in and get something down. Avoid talking with others beforehand about how you will do it or how you interpret a set of themes. Exploring differences of interpretation in your group is part of the activity. ***Do not look ahead to the directions for Step 2 until you have finished your drawing.***

2. When everyone in your group has finished both drawings, share them with each other, explain and interpret them, and talk about your feelings. (*10 to 15 minutes per person*) Following are some points to explore as you share the self-portraits.

How is one drawing of yourself different from the other?

What interpretation did you put on your themes? (Did you interpret "away from work" as "at home"? Or "at play"? Or "having fun"? and so forth.)

Are your portraits consistent with other data the group has about you, expecially with the "I am . . . ." statements?

Did you portray yourself as doing things or as being someone? What does that mean to you?

Did you portray yourself alone or with others? What does this say to you?

What is the relation between the roles you play and the person you are in your drawings?

"A slave is one who waits for someone else to come and free him." Ezra Pound

Constraints

WHAT HOLDS YOU BACK? 60 minutes

61

1. In the first column below, make a list of the 10 most significant constraints in your life. Constraints may be internal or external. They are limitations or obligations which you experience as having an impact on you. (*10 minutes*) **Do not look ahead to Step 2 until you have finished your list.**

	I	C	
1.			
2.			
3.			
4.			
5.			
6.			
7.			
8.			
9.			
10.			

2. When you have completed your list, indicate in the middle column which constraints are imposed (I) and which are chosen (C). In the third column, indicate what, if anything, you are doing or might do about each constraint—either to remove it, to modify it, or to cope with it. (*10 minutes*)

3. Now meet with your group and share your answers and reactions to the following questions. (*10 to 15 minutes per person*)

Which constraints have you accepted and which have you not?

Which constraints are physical?

Which constraints are long-standing and which are recent?

Which constraints will disappear with time?

Are there any old choices which you have assumed you cannot change but really can?

How many had trouble completing the list? How many had a hard time limiting the list to 10?

Do any constraints cause you much anger, fear, worry, anxiety, or energy drain?

Which constraints seem to leave you powerless, trapped?

Are there any constraints which are universal, just part of the human condition?

Which are cultural, ethnic, sexist, regional, institutional?

Out of which constraints have you found or developed compensating strengths?

An inventory

WHAT THINGS
MEAN MOST
TO YOU?

64

1. On the work sheet below, make a list of the 10 tangible, physical objects that mean most to you in your life and work. You do not have to own them or even have use of them. You can just want them or enjoy them. Be specific (instead of listing "clothes," for example, list "my favorite red shirt"). (*5 minutes*)

1. _____

2. _____

3. _____

4. _____

5. _____

6. _____

7. _____

8. _____

9. _____

10. _____

2. Share with your group what you have learned as well as your feelings, surprises, questions, reactions. You may find it useful to read your lists to each other. (*10 minutes*) Below are some questions for reflection, sharing, or both.

Did you list things you need or depend on (eyeglasses) as opposed to things you value (a favorite picture)?

Did you list things you do not own or things nobody can own (a fountain, a mountain, a building, the sea, etc.)?

Did you have trouble completing your list? Or find it hard to leave something off?

How many things are work-oriented and how many are life-oriented?

Would you have written a different list at a different time?

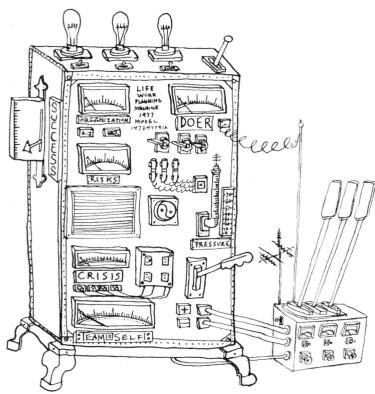

Your work personality

HOW DO YOU WORK BEST?

75 minutes

Here I am 58, and I still don't know what I am going to do when I grow up . . . . the only way to find what you want is to create a job. Nobody worth his salt has ever moved into an existing job.

. . . you know what you don't want to do, but what you do want to do, you don't know. There is no way of finding out but trying . . . . one doesn't marry a job. A job is your opportunity to find out—that's all it is.

. . . I think one of the most important things would be to know if you like pressure or if you cannot take it at all. There may be people who can take pressure or leave it alone, but I have never met any of them. I am one who needs pressure. . . . If there is no deadline staring us in the face, we have to invent one. I am sluggish, lethargic, a lizard, until the adrenalin starts pouring. A low metabolism—psychologically. . . . You have to know whether you belong in a big organization. In a big organization, you don't see results, you are too damn far away from them. The enjoyment is being a part of a big structure . . . . And I think you need to know whether you want to be in daily combat as a dragon- slayer or if you want to think things through, to analyze, prepare. Do you enjoy surmounting the daily crisis, or do you really get your satis- faction out of anticipating and preventing the crisis? These things I believe one does know about oneself at age 20.

There is one great question I don't think most young people can answer: "Are you a perceptive or an analytical person?" This is terribly important. Either you start out with an insight and then think the problem through, or you start out with a train of thought and arrive at a conclusion. One really needs to be able to do both, but most people can't. I am totally unanalytical and completely perceptive. I have never in my life understood anything that I have not seen . . . .

No matter what job it is, it ain't final. The first few years are trials. The probability that the first choice you make is right for you is roughly one in a million. If you decide your first choice is the right one, chances are you are just plain lazy . . . .

Contrary to everything that modern psychologists tell you, I am convinced that one can acquire knowledge, one can acquire skills, but one cannot change his personality. Only the Good Lord changes personality—that's His business. I have had four great children, and I can assure you that by the time they were six months old, they were set in concrete. After six months, parents get educated but not children.

One can take a child and try to bring him out of excessive timidity, but you won't ever make a bold one out of him. Or, one can take a bold one, a rash one, and try to teach him how to count to ten before shooting with the hope that he will count at least to three. But that is all one can do. One can take a charmer and try to get him—charmers are mostly boys—to work to catch up with what he has improvised. And one can get one of those awful, horrible overplanners to jump once in a while. But you are not going to change the basic structure. It is much more important that in this age of psychology people tell the kids that what you are matters, and your values matter . . . .

I am not at all opposed to graduate school per se. I am opposed to graduate school as a delaying action. I am opposed to graduate school as hibernation. And I am opposed to graduate school as education, which it is not . . . . Graduate school is not focused on forming a human being but on imparting a finer set of skills. The purpose is not education, but specialization . . . .

*I am absolutely convinced that one of the greatest needs is the systematic creation of second careers.**

—Peter Drucker

Peter Drucker, in these excerpts and in his many publications, challenges our assumptions about life and work and careers. With his comments in mind, we ask you now to focus on yourself as a working person, to consider your preferences and your personality in a work situation. Locating yourself on the continua that follow and sharing that with the members of your group is a stimulating way to explore some key issues involved in determining the kind of work that best suits you.

---

1. On each of the lines below, place a mark at the point where you see yourself. (*10 minutes*)

Pay particular attention to differences of interpretation around each continuum and to the assumptions you make about what they mean. If you have difficulty understanding a particular item, interpret it as you see fit and move on. To explore these differences of interpretation is part of the learning experience of this activity.

You may find yourself tempted to mark both sides of a given continuum or to put yourself in the middle. Try to resist this temptation and take a stand. Sid Simon jokes that only compulsive moderates place themselves in the middle. If you are puzzled about where you belong, risk the choice that seems best for the moment. As in other activities, this risk of committing yourself may yield the payoff of a good insight.

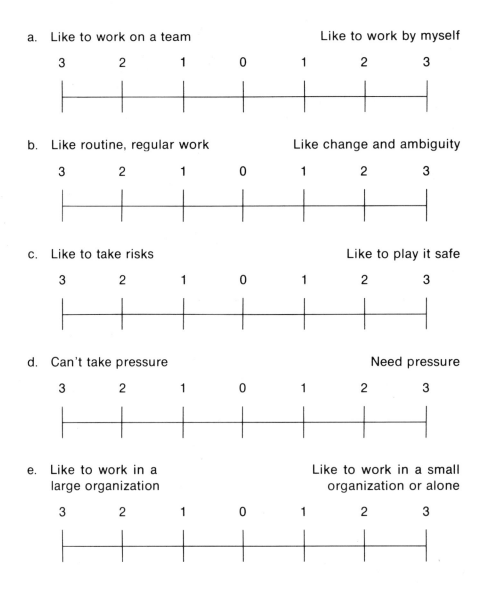

a. Like to work on a team   Like to work by myself

      3   2   1   0   1   2   3

b. Like routine, regular work   Like change and ambiguity

      3   2   1   0   1   2   3

c. Like to take risks   Like to play it safe

      3   2   1   0   1   2   3

d. Can't take pressure   Need pressure

      3   2   1   0   1   2   3

e. Like to work in a   Like to work in a small
    large organization   organization or alone

      3   2   1   0   1   2   3

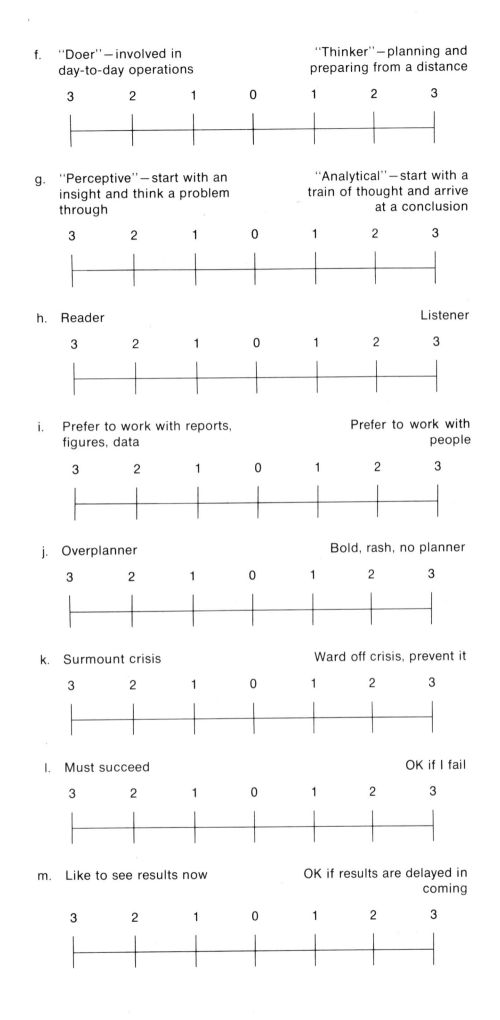

f. "Doer"—involved in
    day-to-day operations

    "Thinker"—planning and
    preparing from a distance

    3   2   1   0   1   2   3

g. "Perceptive"—start with an
    insight and think a problem
    through

    "Analytical"—start with a
    train of thought and arrive
    at a conclusion

    3   2   1   0   1   2   3

h. Reader

    Listener

    3   2   1   0   1   2   3

i. Prefer to work with reports,
    figures, data

    Prefer to work with
    people

    3   2   1   0   1   2   3

j. Overplanner

    Bold, rash, no planner

    3   2   1   0   1   2   3

k. Surmount crisis

    Ward off crisis, prevent it

    3   2   1   0   1   2   3

l. Must succeed

    OK if I fail

    3   2   1   0   1   2   3

m. Like to see results now

    OK if results are delayed in
    coming

    3   2   1   0   1   2   3

2. When your group has completed the questionnaire, share your reactions with each other. There is no need to labor through the entire list exhaustively. Start with the items that interest you or others and follow your interest. (*10 to 15 minutes per person*)

You might open your workbook to the continua pages for comparison and reference. It helps if you mark your positions clearly so that they can be seen easily.

Items are randomly arranged and there is no significance or consistency to the right or left side of zero in the continua.

Below are some questions for reflection, sharing, or both:

Are there any differences in the way people interpreted some continua?

Did people make different assumptions?

Did you put yourself at either extreme on any items? What were the items? What significance does this have for you?

How dependent on present cirsumstances is the way you answered the continua? Would you answer in the same way were circumstances different?

Did you answer from the point of view of how you are or of how you would like to be?

What profiles in your group are similar or dissimilar to yours?

How consistent are your answers with other data produced so far?

How consistent are you within the continua? Which items seem to be related?

Did answering the continua indicate any conflicts or tensions in you? Which were the hardest items for you to answer?

Key relationships

WHO MEANS MOST TO YOU?

90 minutes

. . . our needs from and toward other people are three: inclusion, control, *and* affection. *We achieve interpersonal joy when we find a satisfying, flexible balance in each of these areas between ourselves and other people. Inclusion refers to the need to be with people and to be alone. The effort in inclusion is to have enough contact to avoid loneliness and enjoy people; enough aloneness to avoid enmeshment and enjoy solitude. The fully realized man (sic!) can feel comfortable and joyful both with and without people, and knows with how much of each — and when — he functions best. In the area of* control *the effort is to achieve enough influence so that a man can determine his future to the degree that he finds most comfortable, and to relinquish enough control so that he is able to lean on others to teach, guide, support, and at times to take some responsibility from him. The fully realized man is capable of either leading or following as appropriate, and of knowing where he*

personally feels most comfortable. In affection the effort is to avoid being engulfed in emotional entanglement (not being free to relate without a deep involvement) but also to avoid having too little affection and a bleak, sterile life without love, warmth, tenderness, and someone to confide in. The fully realized man is aware of his needs, and functions effectively not only in close, emotionally involving situations, but also in those of lesser intensity. As in the other two areas, he is able to both give and take, comfortably and joyfully.*

—*William C. Schutz*

For this activity you will need another large sheet of paper and colored felt markers for each person. You may use the space provided below in the Workbook, but the larger sheet of paper will be much more productive for you.

1. Draw a geometric shape (circle, square, triangle, etc.) representing each person who is significant to you in your life, work, or both. In the center of each shape indicate who this person is. Be sure to include a shape for yourself. Include people who are present or absent, living or dead, part of your current or past life, provided they are truly significant. Experiment not only with shapes but also with their size, color, and location on the page to express what each relationship means to you. (*30 minutes*)

---

* William C. Schutz, *Joy—Expanding Human Awareness*, Grove Press, New York, 1967, pp. 18–19. Schutz's is a very strong statement about relationships. Both men and women can be fully realized persons!

2. Now that you have identified the significant others in your life, explore for yourself and with your group any of the following questions that seem relevant to you. (These questions might also suggest additions to your drawing.) (*10 to 15 minutes per person*)

What is it that makes another significant in your life? (Love, responsibility, control, time, trust, fear, advantage, duty, dependence, etc.)

By whom do you feel most included? Excluded?

In which relationships is control an issue? Where are you the leader? Follower? Both?

Do you have enough affection in your life? Toward whom? From whom?

Who is not in your drawing? Anyone who "should" be there but isn't? Anyone whom you want to be but is not?

Is there anybody in your drawing whom you don't really want there—who you wish were not there?

Which relationships are work-oriented? Life-oriented? Both?

Which relationships do you consider "positive" (supporting, trusting, friendly, "good," etc.) and which do you consider "negative" (nonsupportive, threatening, hostile, "bad," etc.)? Did you omit "negative" relationships?

Where is your support system? At work? Away from work? Both? Neither?

Did you name some people by role (boss, secretary, husband, mother, etc.) rather than by name? Which relationships are role relationships?

Which of your needs are being met in your present relationships? Which are not?

Are there any relationships you wish to change or develop? How? Who needs to change or grow? You? The other? Both?

The discovery that you are isolated or that existing relationships are inadequate, superficial, or lacking in some important respect can be moving. It is particularly important here that your group be supportive and that you focus on growth needs or alternative solutions.

Another inventory

WHAT CONDITIONS OF LIFE AND WORK
MEAN MOST TO YOU?

Not another 10-best list! In Bernard Waber's amusing *Nobody is Perfick,* a child suggests that her friend add an eleventh item to her 10-best list of favorite days of the year. The list-maker responds that she cannot have 11 items on her 10-best list. The friend suggests that she make it an 11-best list, but the list-maker cannot do that:

Why not?
    Because I will have to change all of my other ten-best lists to eleven best.
You have other lists?
    *I have lots of other lists. It's one of the ten best things I like to do: make lists.**

Here we suggest one more list that quickly puts you in touch with some values which seem relevant in this probing of your life and work.

1. On the work sheet below, make a list of the 10 conditions that mean most to you in your life and work. You do not have to enjoy them at the present time. You can just want them. (*5 minutes*)

    The point here is not to list what you want to achieve (goals or results), or resources (brains, skills, or strength), or physical things, or individual people, or personal traits.
    Rather, make a list of what you like to work and live with outside of yourself.
    Your list might name such things as the intangible conditions under which you work and live—time, place, atmosphere, conveniences, limitations, freedoms, quality of life and work, relationships. In a word, your circumstances and surroundings. What makes possible the effective utilization of your resources and the achievement of your goals?

---

* Bernard Waber, *Nobody is Perfick,* Houghton Mifflin, Boston, 1971, p. 101.

1. _____

2. _____

3. _____

3. _____

4. _____

5. _____

6. _____

7. _____

8. _____

9. _____

10. _____

2. Share with your group what you have learned as well as your feel-
    ings, surprises, questions, reactions. You may find it useful to read
    your lists to each other. (*10 minutes*) Below are some questions for
    reflection, sharing, or both.

Are there any items on your list which you do not presently enjoy?

Would you have written a different list at a different time?

How many items are work-oriented and how many life-oriented?

How many items have to do with you alone and how many with other
    people?

Did you have trouble finding 10 things? Did you have trouble limiting
    your list to 10?

The diary

WHAT DO YOU WANT TO BE DOING?

90 minutes

I know of no more encouraging fact than the unquestionable ability of man to elevate his life by a conscious endeavor. . . . To affect the quality of the day, that is the highest of arts. Every man is tasked to make his life, even in its details, worthy of the contemplation of his most elevated and critical hour. . . .

I went to the woods because I wished to live deliberately, to front only the essential facts of life, and see if I could not learn what it had to teach, and not, when I came to die, discover that I had not lived. I did not wish to live what was not life, living is so dear; nor did I wish to practise resignation, unless it was quite necessary. I wanted to live deep and suck out all the marrow of life, to live so sturdily and Spartan-like as to put rout all that was not life. . . .

I learned this, at least, by my experiment; that if one advances confidently in the direction of his dreams, and endeavors to live the life which he has imagined, he will meet with a success unexpected in common hours.*

— Henry David Thoreau

---

* Henry David Thoreau, *Walden and Civil Disobedience*, Houghton Mifflin, Boston, 1957, pp. 62 and 220.

It is time to get in touch with your dreams! The diary is a stimulating step into the future, an opportunity to imagine and to feel what life might be like for you on two days several months or years ahead, when you are doing what you want to be doing.

1. Select a point in the future toward which it makes sense, now, to plan your life and work. Somewhere between six months and five years will do. Less than six months is probably too soon to really be future; longer than five years is probably too far off to visualize unless you have some specific target date in mind, like retirement or children going away to school. Select two days at this point in the future, a Friday and a Saturday. Friday is a work day and Saturday is a leisure day. If, for you, another pair of days better suits the purpose, substitute them.

    Write a diary account of each of these two days. Try to put into these two days everything you want. Be as free or as fantastic as you wish to be. Play with the future and explore it. Do not censor. Put down what comes to mind, even if you think you can never have it or do it or if one thing is at odds with another. Go through the whole of each day and be as vivid, concrete, and detailed as you can be. Where are you? What are you doing throughout your day? What's new? How do you feel? Who else is in your life now? (*15 minutes per day*)

If you have some difficulty getting started on the diary because you have yet to make some basic decisions about the future, select an alternative and use the diary to "try it on for size." You are not committed to what you write about; you are experimenting. You might even wish to return to this activity later and try out other alternatives.

DIARY

DATE: FRIDAY, _____

DIARY

DATE: <u>SATURDAY,</u>

2. When you have finished, share your diary with your group. Take some time to share feelings and explore the implications of what you and others have written. (*10 to 15 minutes per person*)

The life work calendar

LOOKING AHEAD TO THE REST OF YOUR LIFE   20 minutes

Often people get so caught up in the pressures of the moment that they lose the broader picture of their life experience. We have developed this calendar to provide a realistic and factual look at what you know about your future, to the extent that it is possible to know anything about it. If things continue on schedule, there will be certain relationships, situations, events, and commitments you can count on. It seems well to have a long-range view of these, and of how they relate to one another, before you move on to making decisions and plans for yourself. Many of us have had extraordinary insights as we took this opportunity to get a clear picture of what the future might look like.

1. The Life Work Calendar is a blank calendar, with each vertical space representing one year. Starting with the current year, write in, on the top horizontal line, succeeding years to the end of the page or to the point beyond which you do not reasonably expect to live. Then, on the next horizontal line, write in your present age in the current year and the age you will be in each succeeding year.

    On successive lines, write in and project the ages of other people who are important to you and to whom you will continue to relate over the years: father, mother, spouse, children, brothers, sisters, relatives, business associates, professional associates, friends, and support people like your physician, attorney, broker, agent, etc.

    On other successive lines, enter the projection of future events, such as education for yourself or others, the mortgage, when children leave home, retirement, institutional events that might affect you, or any other kind of information that seems useful. (*10 minutes*)

85

YEAR	
AGE	

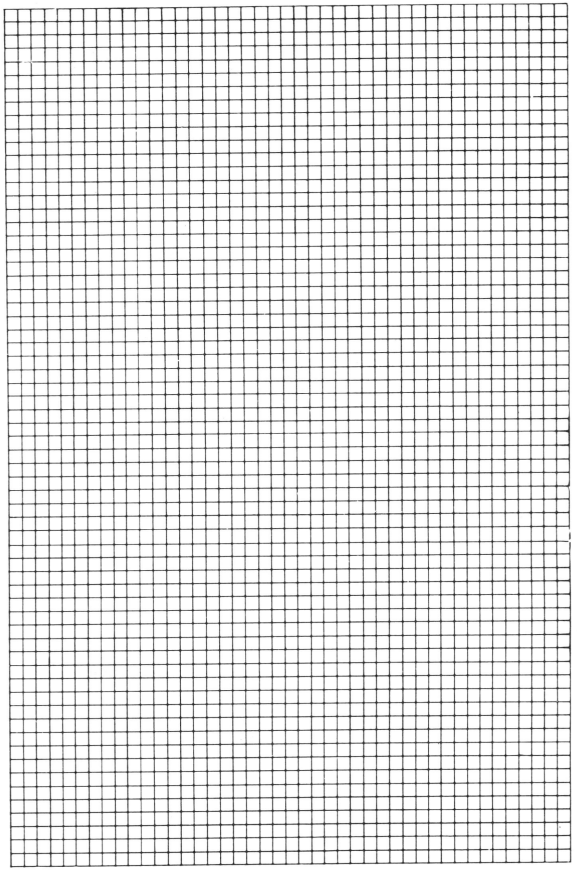

2.   When you have completed your calendar, meet with your group and share your reactions to this activity, using the following questions for reflection, sharing, or both. (*10 minutes*)

Is your life expectancy realistic? Are you avoiding dealing with death?

How many people do you know who are now the age you project for the end of your life? What is the state of their health?

What feelings did you have as you developed your calendar?

Were there any surprises? Did you learn anything? What was it?

George Gray

I have studied many times
The marble which was chiseled for me —
A boat with a furled sail at rest in a harbor.
In truth it pictures not my destination
But my life.
For love was offered me and I shrank from its disillusionment;
Sorrow knocked at my door, but I was afraid;
Ambition called to me, but I dreaded the chances.
Yet all the while I hungered for meaning in my life.
And now I know that we must lift the sail
And catch the winds of destiny
Wherever they drive the boat.
To put meaning in one's life may end in madness,
But life without meaning is the torture
Of restlessness and vague desire —
It is a boat longing for the sea and yet afraid.

Russian Sonia

I, born in Weimar
Of a mother who was French
And German father, a most learned professor,
Orphaned at fourteen years,
Became a dancer, known as Russian Sonia,
All up and down the boulevards of Paris,
Mistress betimes of sundry dukes and counts,
And later of poor artists and of poets.
At forty years, passée, I sought New York
And met old Patrick Hummer on the boat,
Red-faced and hale, though turned his sixtieth year,
Returning after having sold a ship-load
Of cattle in the German city, Hamburg.
He brought me to Spoon River and we lived here
For twenty years — they thought that we were married!
This oak tree near me is the favorite haunt
Of blue jays chattering, chattering all the day.
And why not? for my very dust is laughing
For thinking of the humorous thing called life.*

* Edgar Lee Masters, *Spoon River Anthology,* Collier Books, New York, 1967, pp. 87, 106.

Alexander Throckmorton

In youth my wings were strong and tireless,
But I did not know the mountains.
In age I knew the mountains
But my weary wings could not follow my vision—
Genius is wisdom and youth.

Deacon Taylor

I belonged to the church,
And to the party of prohibition;
And the villagers thought I died of eating watermelon.
In truth I had cirrhosis of the liver,
For every noon for thirty years,
I slipped behind the prescription partition
In Trainor's drug store
And poured a generous drink
From the bottle marked
"Spiritus frumenti."

Margaret Fuller Slack

I would have been as great as George Eliot
But for an untoward fate.
For look at the photograph of me made by Penniwit,
Chin resting on hand, and deep-set eyes—
Gray, too, and far-searching.
But there was the old, old problem:
Should it be celibacy, matrimony or unchastity?
Then John Slack, the rich druggist, wooed me,
Luring me with the promise of leisure for my novel,
And I married him, giving birth to eight children,
And had no time to write.
It was all over with me, anyway,
When I ran the needle in my hand
While washing the baby's things,
And died from lock-jaw, an ironical death.
Hear me, ambitious souls,
Sex is the curse of life!

Abel Melveny

I bought every kind of machine that's known—
Grinders, shellers, planters, mowers,
Mills and rakes and ploughs and threshers—
And all of them stood in the rain and the sun,
Getting rusted, warped and battered,
For I had no sheds to store them in,
And no use for most of them.
And toward the last, when I thought it over,
There by my window, growing clearer
About myself, as my pulse slowed down,
And looked at one of the mills I bought—
Which I didn't have the slightest need of,
As things turned out, and I never ran—
A fine machine, once brightly varnished,
And eager to do its work,
Now with its paint washed off—
I saw myself as a good machine
*That Life had never used.**

Ibid., pp. 145, 70, 80, and 179.

Retrospective

LOOKING BACK ON THE REST OF YOUR LIFE   90 minutes

If you can begin to see death as an invisible, but friendly, companion on your life's journey—gently reminding you not to wait till tomorrow to do what you mean to do—then you can learn to live your life rather than simply passing through it.

Whether you die at a young age or when you are older is less important than whether you have fully lived the years you have had. One person may live more in eighteen years than another does in eighty. By living, we do not mean frantically accumulating a range and quantity of experience valued in fantasy by others. Rather, we mean living each day as if it is the only one you have. We mean finding a sense of peace and strength to deal with life's disappointments and pain while always striving to discover vehicles to make more accessible, increase, and sustain the joys and delights of life. One such vehicle is learning to focus on some of the things you have learned to tune out—to notice and take joy in the budding of new leaves in the spring, to wonder at the beauty of the sun rising each morning and setting each night, to take comfort in the smile or touch of another person, to watch with amazement the growth of a child, and to share in children's wonderfully "uncomplexed," enthusiastic, and trusting approach to living. To live.

To rejoice at the opportunity of experiencing each new day is to prepare for one's ultimate acceptance of death. For it is those who have *not really lived—who have left issues unsettled, dreams unfulfilled, hopes shattered, and who have let the real things in life (loving and being loved by others, contributing in a positive way to other people's happiness and welfare, finding out what things are really you) pass them by—who are most reluctant to die. It is never too late to start living and growing. This is the message delivered each year in Dickens's "Christmas Carol"—even old Scrooge, who has spent years pursuing a life without love or meaning, is able through his willing it, to change the road he's on. Growing is the human way of living, and death is the final stage in the development of human beings. For life to be valued every day, not simply near to the time of anticipated death, one's own inevitable death must be faced and accepted. We must allow death to provide a context for our lives, for in it lies the meaning of life and the key to our growth.* *

—Joseph L. Braga and Laurie D. Braga

We suggest that you take a look at your lifetime goals and values by "looking back on the rest of your life"; that is, by writing about yourself after your death. This is a place you have never been, and you will probably find the perspective unusual and provocative of feeling and insight.

1. Write an account of the rest of your own life. Commit yourself to a date of death. This may not be easy, but it may help to put the activity into sharper focus. (*30 minutes*)

Write your account from the point of view of one who knew you well. Put into it what you would like to have it say. Stretch your account out to include the future as well as the past. What do you want the rest of your life to look like? How do you want to spend the time you have left in life? What do you want to accomplish in your lifetime? What do you want your life to have meant to the world, to colleagues and friends, to family, to yourself? What are the lifetime values with which you want to be identified? What does a lifetime mean to you?

You can write your account in the form of a letter from one friend or relative to another, in the form of a magazine or newspaper profile, or as a eulogy. Try to put down not just facts but also some feelings and some judgments about how you lived your life.

When you have finished, sum up what you have written in a one-line epitaph.

You may find this activity exciting and inspiring. On the other hand, you may find it sad, lonely, threatening, or even frightening. If you feel it would be useful, talk about your feelings with your group at this time.

---

*From the Foreword in Elizabeth Kübler-Ross, *DEATH: The Final Stage of Growth,* © 1975, pp. x, xi. Reprinted by permission of Prentice-Hall, Englewood Cliffs, N.J.

RETROSPECTIVE — LOOKING BACK ON THE REST OF YOUR LIFE

BORN_____

DIED_____

EPITAPH————————————————————————————

2. When you and others in your group have finished, share with each other what you have written. Be sure to give yourselves ample time to deal with feelings which may surface at this point. Be sensitive to people's needs and be supportive of their feelings. (*10 to 15 minutes per person*)

The life work checklist

SUMMING UP

4 hours

Here's a list to end all lists—a list of you! The Life Work Checklist is a summarizing activity—we ask you to sum up *yourself* in a comprehensive list of values, interests, experience, beliefs, etc.

In the Checklist you will recount what you have learned about yourself and may find areas which you have missed, forgotten, or avoided. You will put the learnings and insights gained in the previous activities into a profile of yourself, the base upon which you will later set goals and make decisions and plans.

Sharing the Checklist with your group can provide a rich opportunity for checking out your self-image against the perceptions they have gathered through the previous activities. This can be a very growth-promoting and moving experience.

The Checklist can take a long time, particularly if you choose to use it as a vehicle for feedback. We suggest that you complete your lists and then make a decision in the group about the time you wish to give to the sharing and the method you will follow.

1. Using the Checklist as a scanning device, put down whatever seems significant about yourself in response to each item. Use the work sheets which follow the one-page summary of the Checklist to record your responses. (*90 minutes*)

    What kind of data should you put down? You might record your wants, likes, experiences, motives, feelings, behavior, problems, goals, hopes, fears, values, needs, resources, etc. Almost anything! The point is to put down *your* personal response to each item—a summary profile of who you are. To what you have learned about yourself in Life Work Planning, add how you see yourself and feel about yourself now. Include anything else that seems appropriate.

    If there are subheadings you would like to add, add them. If there are subheadings in one section that you think should go in another, put them there. You may even want to add, delete, or combine headings or subheadings. Do any or all of these. Fill out the Checklist in any sequence which appeals to you.

    Give yourself time to put something down for each subheading. Skip over items to which you have no immediate response. Try to move quickly enough to finish the entire list in a maximum of 1½ hours and come back to items you have skipped or about which you have more to say.

    If you are puzzled about how to get started, you may find the following example helpful:

AGE *42!! Middle-aged, but feel younger than I am.*

STRENGTH *Strong — don't use my strength enough. * Want more physical activity.*

ENERGY LEVEL *Has been higher — feel bogged down. * Anxious to snap out of it — hopeful.*

HEALTH *Generally excellent but age creeping in — a little fearful of that.*

APPEARANCE *Seems to me better than it ever has — important to me.*

PHYSICAL

Age
Strength
Energy level
Health
Appearance
Coordination
Senses
Body awareness
Body image
Sports
Recreation
Touch
Comfort
Pleasure
Pain

EMOTIONAL

Temperament
Awareness of own feelings
  Awareness of others' feelings
Acceptance of own feelings
  Acceptance of others' feelings
Support
Expressiveness
Personal characteristics
Emotional patterns
Mother
Father
Siblings
Motivations — needs and drives
Fears
Defenses
Conflicts
Choice

MATERIAL

Food
Dwelling
Clothing
Things
Possessions
Money
Standard of living
Geographical location
Place
Space
Surroundings
Travel
Nature
Transportation media
Communication media
Place of work
Office

INTELLECTUAL

Ability — what type
Ability — how much
Education
Awareness
Utilization of capabilities
Theoretical — practical
Articulateness
Rigidity — flexibility
Innovation
Reading
Study

OCCUPATIONAL

Talents
Training
Education
Experience
Effort
Success
Failure
Pressure
Interest
Importance
Achievement
Effectiveness
Relevance
Advancement
Recognition
Responsibility
Growth
Supervision
Reward
Colleagues
Working conditions
Status
Security

SPIRITUAL

Ethics
Morals
Religion
Mystical experience
God
Faith
Prayer
Worship
Person
Spirit
Supernatural
Extrasensory experience
Spiritualism

SOCIAL

Warmth
Acceptance by others
Acceptance of others
Rejection
Orientation toward people
Family
Friends
Politics
Intimacy
Initiative
Independence
Control
Dependence
Counterdependence
Interdependence
Approachability
Belonging
Openness
Competition
Trust
Self-confidence
Mannerisms
Prejudices
Justice
Synergy

THE OTHER CATEGORY

Life
Time
Love
Work
Sex
Leisure
Culture
Art
Imagination
Growth
Maturity
Creativity
Freedom
Risk
Joy
Fun
Play
Humor
Happiness
Authenticity
Self-image (positive-negative)
Willingness to change
Retirement
Loneliness
Death

PHYSICAL

Age

Strength

Energy level

Health

Appearance

Coordination

Senses

Body awareness

Body image

Sports

Recreation

Touch

Comfort

Pleasure

Pain

EMOTIONAL

Temperament

Awareness of own feelings

Awareness of others' feelings

Acceptance of own feelings

Acceptance of others' feelings

Support

Expressiveness

Personal characteristics

Emotional patterns

Mother

Father

Siblings

Motivations—needs and drives

Fears

Defenses

Conflicts

Choice

MATERIAL

Food

Dwelling

Clothing

Things

Possessions

Money

Standard of living

Geographical location

Place

Space

Surroundings

Travel

Nature

Transportation media

Communication media

Place of work

Office

INTELLECTUAL

Ability — what type

Ability — how much

Education

Awareness

Utilization of capabilities

Theoretical — practical

Articulateness

Rigidity — flexibility

Innovation

Reading

Study

OCCUPATIONAL

Talents

Training

Education

Experience

Effort

Success

Failure

Pressure

Interest

Importance

Achievement

Effectiveness

Relevance

Advancement

Recognition

Responsibility

Growth

Supervision

Reward

Colleagues

Working conditions

Status

Security

SPIRITUAL

Ethics

Morals

Religion

Mystical experience

God

Faith

Prayer

Worship

Person

Spirit

Supernatural

Extrasensory experience

Spiritualism

SOCIAL

Warmth

Acceptance by others

Acceptance of others

Rejection

Orientation toward people

Family

Friends

Politics

Intimacy

Initiative

Independence

Control

Dependence

Counterdependence

Interdependence

Approachability

Belonging

Openness

Competition

Trust

Self-confidence

Mannerisms

Prejudices

Justice

Synergy

THE OTHER CATEGORY

Life

Time

Love

Work

Sex

Leisure

Culture

Art

Imagination

Growth

Maturity

Creativity

Freedom

Risk

Joy

Fun

Play

Humor

Happiness

Authenticity

Self-image (positive-negative)

Willingness to change

Retirement

Loneliness

Death

2. When you have completed filling out the Checklist, determine in your group how you will share the experience and how much time you will take. There is no need to read through the entire list. You will want to be selective, exploring in your group those categories or items that are of particular interest to you. (*30 minutes per person*)

If you do wish to use this activity to gather feedback from members of your group, we suggest that—before you share what you have written down—you ask for *their* perceptions of you in areas you select. Each member of the group should select the items which have most significance to him or her.

You may find it useful to take one whole category at a time, with all its subheadings, or you may find that skipping around is more functional. Sometimes the categories form a framework within which people find it convenient to say what they had on their minds anyway. In any case it is advisable to limit the amount of time for each person according to the total time you have made available. You might want to review the article on pages 47 and 48, which provides some guidelines that will be useful in a feedback session.

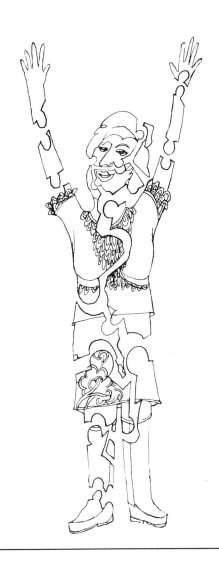

The grid

INTERCONNECTIONS

The focus of Life Work Planning now shifts from gathering information to doing something with it: organizing it, understanding it, making plans, making decisions, taking action.

The checklist produces a comprehensive bank of raw data. The Grid is one means of processing and organizing these data in order to begin the transition from reflection and self-knowledge to action. It will help you to draw together what you have learned about yourself. It will also help you to see useful links between different areas of self-knowledge.

1. Turn to the Grid work sheets on the following pages. In the left-hand column you will find the eight categories from the life work checklist.

Across the top you will find eight headings. Below you will find a list of process questions to guide you in filling out the Grid.

Checklist. . . . What are the most important items for you from each category on the Checklist? Be selective.

I have been. . . . What has been your behavior with regard to each item over the significant past? Go back as far as seems useful. Be specific.

I am. . . . How do you see yourself now with regard to each item? What is your present behavior, attitude, self-image?

I can. . . . What are your capabilities, resources, and potentials with regard to each item?

I need. . . . What are your needs with regard to each item? (Physical needs, physiological needs, safety needs, belonging needs, love needs, self-esteem needs, self-actualization needs.)

I must. . . . What are your constraints with regard to each item? Internal limitations or external circumstances? What do you have to do or not do?

I want. . . . What are your preferences, likes, desires, and objectives with regard to each item? What are the attractive possibilities, options, alternatives for you? Don't worry too much about being realistic. Put down what you want.

I am going to. . . . What action steps are you going to take with regard to each item?

Use everything you have learned about yourself so far to fill in the Grid formed by these two sets of headings. Go back over the work sheets you have already completed, especially those which have been most significant to you, and draw on the information there. But do not limit your thinking to them; also put down what comes to mind now. The example on pages 112 and 113 may be helpful to you.

Give yourself 1 to 1½ hours to fill out the Grid. If you see that you are going to need more time, speed up your work by going through in outline and come back later to fill in the details. Try to get the big picture, the flow. Be selective, especially in the first column, and limit yourself to items of real significance to you. After you have selected your significant items, work each item across the Grid before going on to the next. Let your feelings determine the order in which you work with the items you have selected. Be sure to get the horizontal flow.

As the Grid develops, look for crossovers, interconnections, ways in which Checklist items and the information which flows from them influence each other.

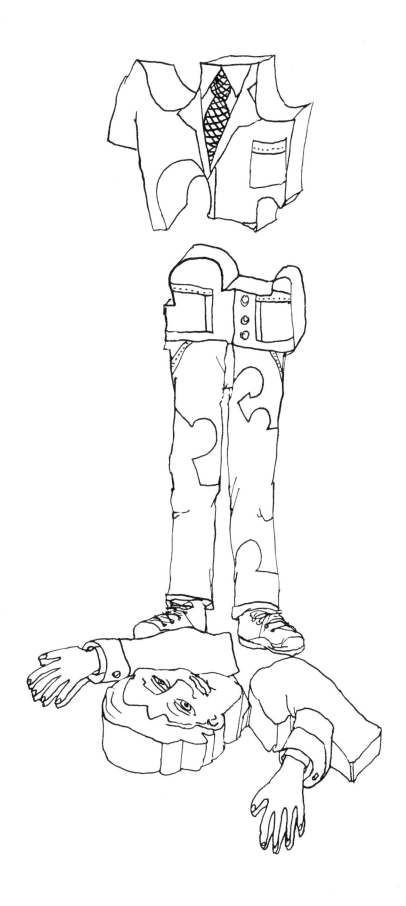

THE GRID

CHECKLIST	I HAVE BEEN . . .	I AM . . .	I CAN . . .
PHYSICAL Strength	Athletic and strong	Strong - not very active. Swim once a week. Office work rather than ski or walk. Activity is w/children - very limited to watching	Be fit and maintain strength. Take time for my activity. Afford to join tennis club.
EMOTIONAL Energy level	Very high energy - wasting time after cocktail hour.	Intense - high energy - too tense and time-pressured	Slow down now. Maintain high energy without tension if I work at it. Cut down on cocktail/wine time.

NEED . . .	I MUST . . .	I WANT . . .	I AM GOING TO . . .
ook, trim and althy.	- - - - - - - - - -	To be more active. To feel better, healthier. To learn to play tennis.	Continue swimming. Take time to walk, play. Join tennis club — take lessons.
nation / pressure / ragement / to usy	Keep up the office work, correspondence, finances, files, administrivia and run the house / home.	To stay young-high energy. To be in touch w/ tensions and grow out of them. To use free time better.	Take time for meditation or prayer or reading. Limit drink occ. wine Channel some energy into new directions in fall. Find regular time for office work.

THE GRID

CHECKLIST	I HAVE BEEN . . .	I AM . . .	I CAN . . .
PHYSICAL			
EMOTIONAL			

I NEED . . .	I MUST . . .	I WANT . . .	I AM GOING TO . . .

CHECKLIST	I HAVE BEEN . . .	I AM . . .	I CAN . . .
MATERIAL			
INTELLECTUAL			

I NEED . . .	I MUST . . .	I WANT . . .	I AM GOING TO . . .

CHECKLIST	I HAVE BEEN . . .	I AM . . .	I CAN . . .
OCCUPATIONAL			
SPIRITUAL			

I NEED . . .	I MUST . . .	I WANT . . .	I AM GOING TO . . .

I NEED . . .	I MUST . . .	I WANT . . .	I AM GOING TO . . .

CHECKLIST	I HAVE BEEN . . .	I AM . . .	I CAN . . .
SOCIAL			
OTHER			

I NEED . . .	I MUST . . .	I WANT . . .	I AM GOING TO . . .

I NEED . . .	I MUST . . .	I WANT . . .	I AM GOING TO . . .

Restatement of your life work situation

WHERE ARE YOU NOW?

1. You may remember that the opening activity of this program was a questionnaire which asked you to focus on your present life work situation, to specify where you saw yourself at that moment and what changes you foresaw.

   We ask you now to take another look at your present situation **without looking back to your earlier statement.** You have now taken many hours to probe into your views of yourself and your circumstances and to explore some directions for the future. This reexpression of your life work situation may reflect some clarity, growth, and change in your perceptions.

   Fill out the following questionnaire. Again, we ask you to be thorough in your thinking but concise and brief in your responses. (*10 minutes*)

122

Briefly describe your life work situation. Your life work situation has two sides: (1) your work—what you do, your job, occupation, work experience, studies, how you make a living; and (2) your life—how you live, your life-style, the quality of your life.

_____

_____

_____

_____

Which concerns you more? Your life? Your work? Both?_____

Why?_____

_____

_____

What is changing in your life and work, and how?

You?_____

Your life circumstances?_____

Your work circumstances?_____

If you are under pressure to do anything about your life or work situation, or both, what is it and when do you have to do it?

_____

_____

_____

2. Now you might like to compare the answers you have just given with the answers you gave to the questions in the "Statement of your Life Work Situation" at the beginning of the program. (*5 minutes*) **Then move directly on to the next activity, Objective Setting.**

Objective setting

WHY DO YOU WANT WHAT YOU WANT? 60 minutes

A critical principle behind the design of this program is that unless our actions and behavior grow out of our objectives for ourselves, unless we identify our own values and goals and act out of them, we are not living our life. Establishing objectives, then, is the next step in the Life Work Planning process.

When establishing objectives for yourself, a key distinction is that between an objective and an activity. An objective is our term for what you achieve by what you do. It is the intended result of your action — the purpose, the goal, the reason why you are doing what you are doing. An activity is what you do, an action step or task.

124

The next step will be to define and develop a list of objectives for yourself. A well-stated objective is:

The intended *result* (purpose, goal, the "why" of your actions)

Specific

Measurable

Expressed in *action* terms ("to" followed by an action verb)

Uniquely *yours* and not someone else's

Within your control

Real (honest)

Realistic (not too easy but not too hard)

In sorting out your objectives, you will note that they relate to each other and that there are levels of objectives. An action undertaken in order to achieve one objective may become an objective in itself with its own set of action steps. In order to have a fulfilling and satisfying career life (objective), one action step might be to complete medical school (activity). At the next level, completing medical school becomes an objective with its own list of action steps (i.e., identifying the school, applying, enrolling, going to classes, doing homework, etc.).

Any one objective is likely to be reached by engaging in more than one activity. If my objective is to make $1 million within the next 10 years, I must do more than draw a good salary; I must invest my earnings, find a multiple market, sell out at the appropriate time, and perhaps even murder my grandmother! Similarly, a single activity can have many objectives. A major-league baseball player might play to make money, to become famous, to excel at something, and to have fun.

Life can be lived out of your values, needs, and interests. Or it can be a series of activities unrelated to your deeper self. Our hope here is that you can make the effort to identify the objectives that will give your next year, next decade, or entire lifetime meaning for you. We hope that, by identifying the result you intend for your activity, you may have the satisfaction of achieving results that are congruent with your deepest values. We ask that you take time now to make yourself a list of objectives, filtering out activities, reworking, correcting, and adding according to the criteria listed above. Give each its own target date for achievement.

1. In the first column on the next page, list what goals and objectives you have identified for your life, work, or both. In the second column, make a list of the actions you plan in the future to reach your goals and realize your objectives. A good source for these is the "I want to . . ." and "I am going to . . ." columns of the Grid, but do not limit yourself to them. (*15 to 30 minutes*)

OBJECTIVES	TARGET DATE	ACTIVITIES

2. Next, look at the objectives and activities on your list, and make sure that you have not confused them with each other. By far the most common confusion is putting activities or the completion of activities on your objective list (to finish school). The way to test if each item on your objectives list is really an objective and not an activity is to ask why you want to do that, or what result you intend to achieve by doing what you propose to do. (Why do you want to finish school? To earn more money? To have the satisfaction of knowing you can do it? To qualify yourself for a profession or job? These are all possible objectives for the activity "finishing school.") (*10 minutes*)

3. When you have completed your list of objectives, we ask that you meet with your group to share it. (*15 to 30 minutes*) Consider the following questions as part of this sharing:

Are your objectives consistent with the insights you have gained in earlier Life Work Planning activities?

Do your objectives avoid dealing with any challenging issues you raised earlier?

PHASE II

Putting it all together

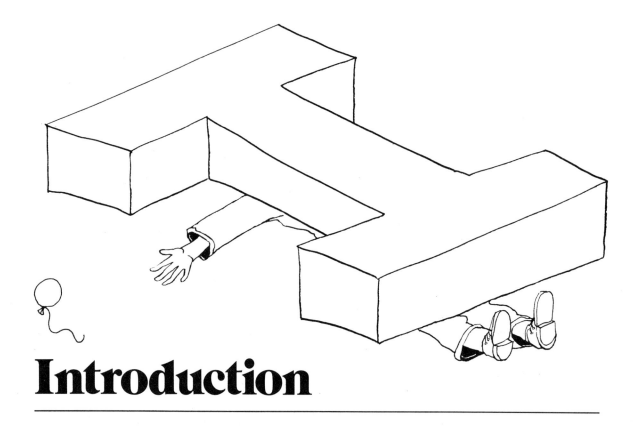

Introduction

You have now completed Phase I of Life Work Planning. The activities so far have focused on self-awareness. A more accurate and complete picture of yourself is a result in itself. But Life Work Planning does not stop at self-awareness. In Phase II you ask a different kind of question. Now that you know what you know about yourself, what are you going to do about it? Where are you going from here?

The closing activities of Phase I have begun the shift from self-awareness to action. In the Checklist you summarized and organized the fragmented insights of earlier activities into the perspective of your whole person. In the Grid you looked for directions, interconnections, trends, indications of priority areas for action. In the Restatement of your Life Work Situation you concentrated on results which are important to you—short-range, mid-range, and long-range.

Now that you have identified these results, you may want to make decisions and plans to achieve them, and you may need to deal with obstacles in your path. Each of the activities in Phase II offers a process for organizing information so that your decisions and plans may fully and accurately reflect your objectives and the realities of your particular situation. Which process you use depends on your specific situation.

PROJECT PLANNING

If you are laying out a definite course of action over time which you can visualize as a series of steps, one following another, the best approach will be Project Planning. Planning is clearly useful when you build something; organize an event or a trip; engineer a job shift for yourself; plan a school semester; get started in a new job situation; take off weight; organize a business, government, or community project; run a promotion or sales campaign; etc. All these situations have in common the laying out of a set course of action to achieve a goal.

DECISION MAKING

If you are trying to make a choice among alternatives, you will need the decision-making process. To justify the time and effort involved in using this tool, your choice should be complex, difficult, or important enough: choosing a house, a job, a career, a person, a product or service, a way to do something, etc. Choosing a dessert and choosing a house are both decision-making situations—to use the full process on the former would be overkill.

If there are no existing alternatives or if the existing alternatives are not satisfactory, you may have to either search for or invent new ones or modify existing ones.

Even if there are no alternatives visible to you yet (no jobs available, for example), you can still be in a decision-making situation. Start the process by clarifying your constraints (what a job must give you) and your objectives (what you want out of a job) as a guide in your search for alternatives and in your assessment of them as they come along.

Sometimes choosing one alternative will eliminate others (one house, car, job, candidate, etc.). Sometimes you think that one alternative will not be adequate. You can then choose the best parts of different alternatives (programs, designs, equipment, resource people, etc.). You can combine them in a unique way, building a new tailor-made alternative as you do.

Your decision-making situation may be to choose an alternative to recommend to someone else for decision. This is a valid application of the tool.

Salespersons or others offering services to clients are in the unique position of offering alternatives to meet the objectives of other people. To involve themselves in the client's decision-making process will generally be more productive than simply to engage in selling them an alternative.

If you think that you are in a decision-making situation, double check to see if you have not already really made a choice or if someone else has really made the choice for you. If the choice has been made, you should probably be using Project Planning or Force Field Analysis. If your choice is not final but you favor one alternative, then Decision Making is the right tool.

FORCE FIELD ANALYSIS

Force Field Analysis can be used for two purposes. First, you can use it to test the feasibility of a goal or course of action. Should you go back to work? Should you become a doctor? Should you build a house? Should you get married? and so on. You have mixed feelings about whether the goal or course of action is realistic, attainable, or workable. You are not yet fully committed. You want to diagnose what is involved, to weigh the pros and cons. You want to see if you can make it work. You want to make a go/no-go decision. You are *not* at the moment considering alternatives (or you would be in Decision Making).

Second, you can use it to plan certain types of growth situations which do not fit the Project Planning tool very well: developing a relationship, resolving a conflict, growing in self-confidence, overcoming a tendency to get angry and pop off.

In none of these situations will your plan look like a project, with steps laid out on a time frame. Action steps there will surely be, but who can anticipate everything a spouse or friend or associate will do in sequence? Who can reduce personal or interpersonal growth to a set series of steps to be undertaken? Planning, yes, but your plan will concentrate more on analysis of the positive and opposing forces involved and with how you can best use your resources to deal with them. Your plan will tend to be more tentative—an approach, a strategy, a "game plan," highly responsive to change in yourself and in others.

IDEA BUILDING

Project Planning and Force Field Analysis will each turn up the need to establish action steps to overcome thorny difficulties. The way clear of these difficulties sometimes requires innovative thinking, new ideas, new approaches. Decision Making may clarify your criteria of choice but not give you adequate alternatives. Again, you will have to resort to creative thinking to modify existing alternatives or invent new ones. Idea Building provides a systematic way of collecting and building new ideas to solve the problems of Planning and Decision Making.

Each tool in Phase II is presented with work sheets and detailed, step-by-step briefings on how to use them. Each step of the briefing corresponds to the numbered steps on the work sheet. Of particular value are the process questions, designed to guide the flow and structuring of information in the most useful form. You may find it useful to copy the work sheet headings out on a large sheet of paper or on several sheets of paper for recording your answers to the process questions. When you have decided which process seems appropriate for your situation, take a few minutes to read the briefing to see how it works.

The classic applications of the Phase II tools mentioned above and illustrated on the chart opposite are relatively easy to identify.

A SAMPLING OF POSSIBLE APPLICATIONS OF PHASE II TOOLS

Force Field Analysis	Decision Making	Project Planning	Idea Building
Test feasibility of a goal or course of action, or plan a personal growth situation.	Choose among alternatives.	Lay out an action sequence to achieve a goal.	Find a new idea, approach, alternative or solution.
I've always wanted to be a doctor, but. . . .	Choose a career: doctor, lawyer, etc.	Become a practicing physician in eight years.	How to raise enough money for medical school.
I'd like to become a manager in two years, but. . . .	Choose among jobs A, B, and C.	Become expert in a particular technical field in two years.	How to get my boss to see I can do the job.
Is it feasible for me to build my house?	Choose a building site, an architect, or a design.	Lay out a construction plan.	How to avoid a drainage problem from the hill above.
I'd like to go back to work, but. . . .	Select among jobs A, B, and C.	Relocate with a new job in two years.	Invent a job alternative that is right for me.
I'd like to go into business for myself, but. . . .	Choose the best business venture.	Set up a small business over the next 12 months.	How to resolve some specific difficulty in my new business (raise $10,000).
I'd like to make this relationship work by the end of six months, but. . . .	Should I stay married, get a divorce, or what?	Move out on my own.	How to work out a specific difference (get my need for security met with an insecure partner).
I'd like to finish college, but. . . .	Choose a major field of study.	Plan the school year.	How to get practical experience to match my school training.
I'd like to get myself three hours a day clear, but. . . .	Choose the best activity for my free time.	Develop skill in a productive activity.	How to find space for a workshop.
I'd like to retire early, but. . . .	Select best place for a retirement home.	Plan to set up a part-time small business on my own.	How to cope with a health problem.
I'd like to build a better working relationship with my boss, but. . . .	Choose a project to present to my boss.	Plan a project to propose to my boss.	How to revitalize my dull job.

There are situations for which the appropriate process is not obvious. It may be difficult to distinguish whether you are in a planning or a decision-making situation. Planning presumes a certain amount of decision making. It is premature to plan a trip until you have decided where you are going, when, and for how long. Even when you have resolved these decisions and have started to plan, there may be further decisions to make within your plan, like choice of hotels or itinerary. Planning and decision making are interconnected but separate functions which must be done separately because they involve different processes.

A particularly subtle example of this distinction is the difference between designing a house and planning its construction. Although a design is commonly referred to as a plan (an architect's plan or a blueprint) most designing amounts to inventing and choosing among alternatives many times over—that is, multiple decision making. Planning involves laying out a course of action over a time sequence. The architect chooses (decides on style, size, materials, fixtures, etc.) and the contractor plans (lays out the action sequence for) the construction of the house.

"Should I or shouldn't I . . ." and "Whether or not . . ." situations can be confusing. They narrowly state the situation in terms of one goal or course of action and a negative. This almost never truly represents the situation facing you. The following example illustrates the point. "Should I promote Joe or not?" really means either "I'd like to promote Joe, but . . ." or "Should I give the job to Joe, Harry, or Dick?"

"I'd really like to promote Joe, but . . ." indicates ambivalence; preference along with reservation. This goal or course of action needs analysis for feasibility. What are its pros and cons? This is the function of Force Field Analysis.

"Should I give the job to Joe, Harry, or Dick?" indicates a choice among alternatives. The proper tool to use here is Decision Making.

	Force Field Analysis	Decision Making
Should I become a doctor or not?	I've always wanted to be a doctor, but. . . .	Should I go into medicine, law, business, etc.?
Should I go into business for myself or not?	I want to go into business for myself, but. . . .	Should I go into business A, B, or C?
Should I move to the country or not?	I'd really like to move to the country, but. . . .	Should we move to location A, B, or C?
Should I go back to work or not?	I want to go back to work, but. . . .	Should I take job A, B, or C?
Should I take the promotion or not?	I'd like to take this promotion, but. . . .	Should I take job A, B, or C?

These processes are not simply mechanical devices for one-time use. They do not substitute for your judgment. They marshall the facts so that your judgment is informed, balanced, thorough, and in accord with your values. Planning and Decision Making are lifetime processes that continue over the years and develop with your perception of yourself and the world around you. While you can use only one process at a time, you might over a long period of time use them all many times over.

Now that you have a better idea about how the tools of Phase II work, go back to your list of objectives from the previous activity. Select the ones that seem to merit further analysis. Restate them on the work sheet below, and indicate which tools seem to you the most appropriate. Then proceed to the tools in question and apply them to your objectives.

OBJECTIVES	TARGET DATE	TOOL

Project planning

Project Planning is the process of laying out a course of action to achieve a goal; it is a process for getting from here to there by a specific time.

Planning is commonly thought of as little more than tasks, responsibilities, and costs set out on a time schedule — that is, as a list of who is going to do what, when, and at what cost. Thorough planning takes in several other steps included here.

Following is a summary of process questions and directions to guide you in each step of the Project Planning work sheet which follows. The questions correspond to numbered steps on the work sheet. Make sure you have answered each question that applies to your situation at each step and recorded your answer on the work sheet. There is a sample work sheet on pages 140 and 141 for you to refer to. If you find that the work sheets do not give you enough room, copy out the headings on a large sheet of paper or on several sheets of paper.

1. **Statement of your planning situation.** What is the overall goal or end result you wish to achieve by executing this plan? What are the target dates for beginning and completion?

2. **Objectives of the plan.** What are the specific results you wish to realize by the tasks and activities you will list in Step 7?

- Objectives spell out in detail what you mean by your goal.

- Objectives are not milestones. Milestones are dates when action steps are completed. Objectives are results that action steps achieve when completed.

- Double check to see that each of your objectives states a result and not an action step, task, or activity. Action steps are what you do to achieve objectives. Confusing the two is the most common mistake people make in planning.

- Objectives should be specific, identifying a single key result.

- Objectives should be expressed in action terms, using the word *to* followed by an active verb (*to establish, to maximize, to minimize, to optimize, to avoid*, etc.).

- Objectives should be measurable and—when possible—quantified.

- Be sure to include long-range as well as short-range objectives when appropriate.

3. **Assumptions.** What are the factors that may affect your plan as it unfolds—factors about which there is some degree of uncertainty or probability? Indicate the degree of probability that they will affect your plan. High, medium, low?

   - Your plan is as sound as your assumptions. A plan based on too many assumptions may be a high-risk plan.

   - Can you verify whether or not your assumptions are valid? How? You may want to make verifying an assumption an action step in Step 7. Limiting assumptions which you verify as certain become constraints (Step 5).

4. **Resources.** What do you have available to carry out the purpose of your plan and what do you need to carry out the purpose of your plan?

   - Resources include money, people, machines, materials, time (work hours or work days), capabilities, good name, experience, energy, etc.—anyone or anything available to you.

5. **Constraints.** What are the limitations within which you have to work to achieve your goal?

   - Constraints may be limitations within you or in your resources.

   - They may also be outside circumstances or forces opposing your plan.

   - Test to see if any of your constraints are really only assumptions.

6. ***Key unresolved decision points.*** What are the important decisions affecting your plan that have not yet been made?

   • Key decisions may have to be made by you or by others.

   • Decide what steps you are going to take to resolve each decision. Resolving a decision may become a task in Step 7.

7. ***Tasks or action steps.*** What activities have to be undertaken to achieve the goal of your plan? How long will each take? Who will do each? How will you budget for each task?

8. ***Schedule.*** Which tasks have to be done in sequence? Which can be done in parallel?

   • The bar chart is a blank calendar. Fill in your time units (hours, days, weeks, or months) across the top.

   • Enter your tasks by number in the appropriate blocks, showing their duration, sequence, interrelation, and the critical path (the longest necessary sequence of tasks).

   • Be sure to allow adequate lead time.

   • Make sure your deadlines are realistic.

9. ***Potential problems.*** What might go wrong with your plan? Risky assumptions? Constraints? Approvals? Interruptions? Cost? Time? Complexity? Inexperience? Change? Opposition? Unpredictability?

10. ***Preventive actions.*** What actions can you take to keep these problems potential?

11. ***Contingent actions.*** What actions can you take to minimize the impact of these problems if they become actual?

    • Be sure to add preventive and contingent action steps to your list of tasks in Step 7 and work them into your schedule, Step 8.

PITFALLS IN USING PLANNING

   • Using planning where Force Field Analysis or Decision Making would be more appropriate.

   • Starting to plan before enough basic decisions have been made to make planning practical.

   • Mistaking tasks, action steps, or milestones for objectives.

   • Mistaking assumptions for constraints.

- Failing to give enough attention to what can go wrong with your plan (overreliance on plan).

- Failing to work preventive and contingent actions into your plan.

- Failing to get approvals and decisions from other people.

- Not allowing adequate lead time.

PROJECT PLANNING

1. STATEMENT OF PLANNING SITUATION *Plan to move to area of new job, out of state.* TARGET DATE *September 1, 4 months from now.*

2. OBJECTIVES OF THE PLAN

   To minimize cost of move.
   To minimize strain on self and family.
   To minimize disruption of work/school/vacation.
   To plan but postpone, not really needed.
   To be settled by Aug. 15, (see for vacation
   To minimize dependence on auto travel
   To minimize travel time to work } *Objective for decision making, choosing a home,*
   To maximize job opportunity for spouse) *most for planning a move.*
   To minimize time away from family during move.
   To maximize involvement of family in move.
   To minimize adverse effect on mother in town we are leaving.

3. ASSUMPTIONS

	DEGREE OF PROBABILITY
Can sell by June 30	High
Can buy by June 30	Low

4. RESOURCES

HAVE	NEED
Partial payment for move	Information about:
Contacts for:	Communities
Real estate agent - new town	Schools
Local accommodations	Services
Super broke real estate	
(in old home (Jane)	
Marketable house	
40% equity in present house	
$4000 contingency fund	
New job - job security	
30% salary increase	

5. CONSTRAINTS

   Must start new job Sept. 1
   Must close on new house by 6/30.
   Must close on old house before 6/30.
   Family can afford only one trip to new town before move.
   Dog must go with us.
   Can't make offer on new house before selling old.

6. KEY UNRESOLVED DECISION POINTS

Choose:	WHOSE DECISION
Mover	myself
Attorney	myself
Bank	myself
Real estate agent	myself + spouse
Community school	family
House	family
Sell or keep piano.	family

7. TASKS OR ACTIONS STEPS

#	Tasks or Actions Steps	TIME REQUIRED	WHOSE RESPONSIBILITY	COST
1.	Put present house on market.	1 day	myself	
2.	Close on old house.	1/2 day	myself & spouse	
3.	Decide real estate agent for new house.		myself	
4.	House hunt.	7 weeks	family	$500
5.	Decide on new house.		family	
6.	Arrange financing.	1 day	myself	
7.	Close on new house.	1 day	self & spouse	$20,000
8.	Arrange telephone/utilities.	Phone calls	spouse	$2,000
9.	Clean up and repair new home.	4 weeks	family, contractors	
10.	Research schools.	1 week	family	
11.	Choose schools.		family	
12.	Register for schools.	2 hours	family	
13.	Sort out possessions.	10 weeks	family	
14.	Pack.	2 weeks	family & movers	
15.	Decide mover.	3 days	myself & spouse	$200
16.	Load.	1 day	family & movers	$1,500
17.	Move.	2 days	family & movers	
18.	Unload.	1 day	family & movers	$1,000
19.	Unpack.	2 weeks	family	
20.	Family trips to new city.	5 days	family	$1,000
21.	Write town for town reports.	2 hours	family	
22.	Get copies of local newspaper.	2 hours	family	
23.	Vacation.	2 weeks	family	
24.	Choose attorney.	2 days	myself	

9. POTENTIAL PROBLEMS — WHAT MIGHT GO WRONG?

Might not be able to buy by 6/30.

PREVENTIVE ACTIONS

25. Get to many real estate agents, use several. Replace steps 3.
26. Alert company to my need for housing.
27. Prepare objectives for house immediately.
28. Visit area, pen-to-learn up alternative ways of locating a home — contact listings, local publications, obituaries, etc.
29. Decide on community as soon as possible. Finding step 11 earlier than scheduled. Advance step 20.

CONTINGENT ACTIONS

Temporary short term furnished rental and storage.
Temporary long term rental (1 year) and buy.
Temporary long term rental and build. Borrow a house.

8. SCHEDULE

	May	June	July	August
Sell old house	1 ③④ ②⑥ ②① ②② ②④ ②⑦ ②③	⑤② ⑦⑧⑨ 2	⑭	
Buy new house	15 ⑬	24		
Move		16 17 18 ⑲		㉓
School	⑩ ⑪ 29		12	

PROJECT PLANNING

1. STATEMENT OF PLANNING SITUATION _____

    _____ TARGET DATE _____

2. OBJECTIVES OF THE PLAN

3. ASSUMPTIONS   DEGREE OF
                                                             PROBABILITY

4. RESOURCES

    HAVE   NEED

5. CONSTRAINTS

6. KEY UNRESOLVED DECISION POINTS   WHOSE
                                                                  DECISION

7. TASKS OR ACTIONS STEPS	TIME REQUIRED	WHOSE RESPONSIBILITY	COST

8. SCHEDULE

9. POTENTIAL PROBLEMS—   PREVENTIVE   CONTINGENT
     WHAT MIGHT GO WRONG?   ACTIONS   ACTIONS

Decision
making

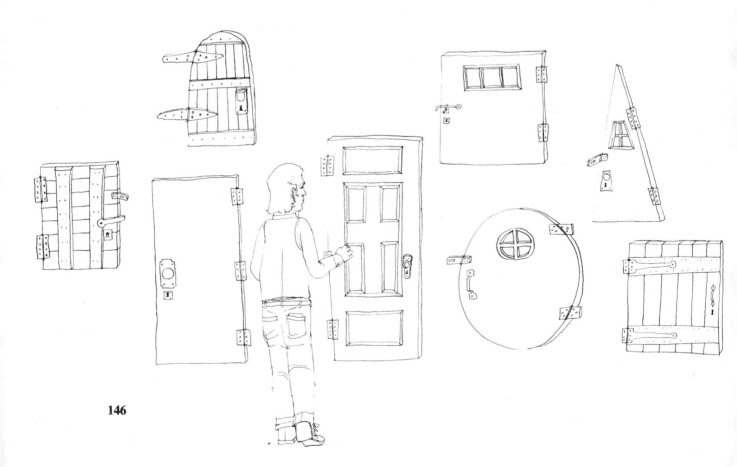

Decision Making, as very precisely understood in this activity, is the process of making a choice among alternatives based on the results or objectives you want to achieve.

Following is a summary of process questions and directions to guide you in each step of the Decision Making work sheet which follows. The questions correspond to numbered steps on the work sheet. Make sure you have answered each question that applies to your situation at each step and recorded your answer on the work sheet. You may find the example on pages 154 and 155 helpful. If you find that the work sheets do not give you enough room, copy out the headings on a large sheet of paper or on several sheets of paper.

1. ***Statement of decision-making situation.*** What alternatives are you choosing among?

   - Since Decision Making is choosing among alternatives, the statement of your decision-making situation should indicate what you are choosing among: to choose the best job, car, house, person, location, product, service, career, method, way of doing something, program, approach, sequence, design, combination, component, etc. Your goal is to choose the best . . . what?

   - This may sound simple, but stating a decision-making situation accurately can be confusing. It is also important, since this process will not work for you unless your starting point is clear.

   - The most important thing is to make sure you are not mixing up different ranges of alternatives and therefore different decisions that should be made separately. Sort them out and make them one at a time. Choosing from among available houses may be preceded by other choices, each with its own range of alternatives: choosing among different sections of the country (West Coast, New England, Southwest, etc.), among locales (cities, towns, regions), and among local neighborhoods or communities. It makes no more sense to compare cities with neighborhoods or homes with towns than it does to compare apples with oranges.

     There are many situations in which it is easy to mix up different sets of alternatives and therefore different decisions. Choosing among careers is not the same as choosing among schools, programs of study, or jobs; choosing among modes of transportation is not the same as choosing among vehicles or cars; choosing to build, rent, or buy and choosing among architects, sites, or designs are different choices; to choose among solutions to a problem is not to choose a way to implement a solution. Each different range of alternatives requires a separate decision.

- You should also be clear as to whose decision this is and, if shared, what your share in the decision-making process is to be. Is it your decision? Someone else's? A shared decision? Should the choice be meeting only your objectives or someone else's as well? The decision should include the objectives of all involved in the decision.

2. **Nonnegotiable constraints on your choice.** What must an alternative do for you or avoid for you before you will consider it? What are the nonnegotiable results you must achieve or avoid in making your choice? What are the firm, fixed requirements—the absolute, mandatory limits on your choice? Be sure that every constraint is really mandatory.

   - Constraints may be imposed (for example, $8,000 may be all you have to spend) or chosen (you may be unwilling to spend more than $8,000). They may be welcome or unwelcome.

   - Be specific about time, places, quantities, costs—in a word, the limits of any constraints. If you cannot measure a constraint, you cannot know if an alternative meets it. Try to quantify constraints if possible.

   - If constraints are too many or too severe, you will have few or no alternatives. Be realistic. Keep them to a minimum.

   - The function of a constraint is to screen out alternatives which do not fall within the limits you set yourself in the situation. When an alternative fails to meet any one constraint, you eliminate it ("no go"; Step 7). When it meets all your constraints, you put it in the running to compare with other alternatives ("go"). There is nothing in between "go" and "no go." An alternative cannot qualify more or less; either it does or it does not.

3. **Objectives.** Within your constraints, what are the results that you want in making this choice? What are your standards of judgment or criteria for comparing alternatives and choosing among them?

   - The function of a constraint is to screen out alternatives which do not qualify and to identify those which do; the function of an objective is to give a basis for comparing alternatives which do qualify. An alternative either meets a constraint or it does not; an alternative can meet an objective more or less well. Constraints are nonnegotiable; objectives are negotiable. You will make trade-offs in meeting objectives—more of one for less of another (for example, more space for greater cost).

   - The difference between a constraint and an objective is not that constraints are more important than objectives. You may not even want a given constraint or think that it is important, but you can still be bound by it. Objectives can be more important to you or more valued by you than the constraints which bind you; although you could buy a safer car for more money than you can afford, this does not mean that your cost constraint is more important to you than safety.

- Formulate objectives with the word *to* followed by an action verb (*maximize, minimize, optimize, avoid, establish,* etc.).

- Objectives should be specific and should state only one key result at a time.

- Be clear how you are going to measure how well each alternative meets any given objective. Quantify objectives when possible, so that you can quantify your measurement. Subjective measurements (on matters of taste, for instance) are OK if you are clear about them.

- Do not list specific features of alternatives as objectives. Reserve them for Step 9. Your list of objectives gives the profile of your values, needs, and desires. A list of features gives the profile of an alternative—that is, it indicates how well it meets your objectives.

    Air-conditioning is a feature of a car. If you consider it mandatory, it is a constraint: you will not consider a car without it. If it is not mandatory, then why do you want it? To maximize comfort? If so, then your objective is to maximize comfort. Air-conditioning and other features like bucket seats and tinted windshields might or might not also contribute to the maximization of comfort.

- Check to see whether there are any elements or concerns (cost) which give you both a constraint (e.g., an alternative *must* cost less than $8,000 to qualify) and an objective (to minimize cost below $8,000).

- Objectives can state contrasting or contradictory values. Trying to get the best quality for the least cost is an attempt to meet two very different objectives. Try to resolve the conflict not by washing out one objective but by finding a good, creative alternative.

4. **Weight the objectives.** How important to you is each objective, and how will you weight it?

- Use a 1-to-10 base in weighting. Give the most important objective(s) a weight of 10. You can have more than one objective weighted 10.

- Go through the rest of your list and ask, with regard to each objective in turn, "Is this objective more, equally, or less important than the previous one?" Assign descending weights accordingly. You might find this easier to do if you first identify your objectives as high, medium, or low in importance to you.

- Use your best judgment in assigning weights, so as to reflect realistically the relative importance of the different objectives on your list.

5. *Alternatives.* What are your known alternatives?

- List each alternative in a separate column on the work sheet.

- Always list the status quo (the way things are; the current alternative if there is one; the present job, house, etc.) as an alternative. It is the alternative about which you have the best information. If you choose something else, you want to be sure it is better than what you have.

- You may think that one alternative alone will not meet your objectives well enough. You will then want to choose the best parts of different alternatives. List the alternatives separately and select the combination of features from different alternatives which best meet your important objectives. This may result in a new and unique or hybrid alternative.

- Where do alternatives come from? Some already exist. You can combine parts of existing alternatives in new ways. You can invent the ideal alternative and work back to reality. You can look at what other people do. You can ask others to help you find one. You can invent one from your objectives. (See Idea Building, below.)

6. *Evidence.* What is the evidence that each alternative does or does not meet every constraint?

- Give specific data on the basis of which you can screen out alternatives which fail to meet your constraints (dates, times, costs, specifications, etc.).

- If you do not have sharp enough information, go get it.

7. *Go/no go.* Are there any alternatives which fail to meet your constraints and which, therefore, you are going to screen out of consideration ("no go")? Which alternatives do meet your constraints ("go")?

- Eliminate the "no-go" alternatives.

- Double check your constraints here. Are you willing or able to change any? This may be necessary if you have too few alternatives.

- Beware of being foolishly rigid about eliminating alternatives that only slightly exceed your constraints. Use your head. Maybe you can alter your constraints slightly.

- There is no need to develop Steps 8 and 9 for alternatives you have eliminated ("no-go" alternatives).

8. **Evidence.** What is the evidence that indicates how well each "go" alternative meets each individual objective? What are the good or bad features of each alternative?

    - In the space provided, record these features and other relevant information. There may be more than one feature relative to any given objective.

    - Record only hard information (dates, times, costs, specifications, etc.) in column 8, not just opinion (OK, pretty good, great, poor, awful, etc.).

    - You may be forced to resort to data which is based on assumption, probability, estimates, or opinion. Realize that such data weaken the assurance that your decision will be a good one.

9. **Estimate.** How well do the features of each alternative satisfy each objective? Indicate level of satisfaction by using the following code: H = high, M = medium, L = low, ? = don't know.

10. **Compare — make tentative choice.** How well does each alternative compare to the others in meeting your overall list of objectives? Where are the trade-offs?

    - Concentrate on those alternatives which do the best job of meeting your high-weighted objectives.

    - See where you are willing to make trade-offs in meeting objectives—more of one for less of another (more interesting work for less compensation).

    - If there are several comparable alternatives, do not fall into the trap of making the choice on the basis of only one objective ("Aw shucks, let's take the cheapest . . . .").

    - If two or more alternatives look equally good, pay particular attention to Step 11.

11. **Test for risk.** What can go wrong if you choose each alternative which now seems favorable to you?

    - List the specific negative consequences.

    - Risk is the combination of seriousness and probability. Assess the risk by indicating how serious each consequence is (H = high, M = medium, L = low, ? = don't know), and how probable each consequence is (H = high, M = medium, L = low, 0 = zero, ? = don't know).

    - Get the data you need to answer the questions you cannot answer at this time.

- See if you can reduce the risk. You may be able to reduce its probability (good housekeeping will prevent a fire) or its seriousness (fire insurance will replace the house). Be sure to figure out the cost of reducing risk and add it to the cost of the alternative.

12. *Final choice.* What is the alternative that best meets your objectives with the minimum level of risk?

PITFALLS IN USING DECISION MAKING

- Using it where you have already made a decision. If you have, act on it. Plan, perhaps.

- Overkill. Using it on situations that are too simple.

- Not separating out different decisions and making them one at a time.

- Using "Should I or shouldn't I . . . ." or "Whether or not . . . ." statements of the purpose of your decision. This is starting the decision-making process by looking at an alternative, not at results.

- Having too many constraints.

- Putting features of alternatives into your objectives.

- Missing objectives.

DECISION MAKING

1. STATEMENT OF DECISION-MAKING SITUATION: TO CHOOSE THE BEST *job*

2. NONNEGOTIABLE CONSTRAINTS	5. ALTERNATIVE A *Quality control inspector at food processing plant*		5. ALTERNATIVE B *County Board of Health Inspector*		5. ALTERNATIVE C *Editor of technical manuscripts for a periodical*		5. ALTERNATIVE D	
	6. EVIDENCE	7. GO/NO GO	6. EVIDENCE	7. GO/NO GO	6. EVIDENCE	7. GO/NO GO	6. EVIDENCE	7. GO/NO GO
Minimum daily rate $40	$38 per day for this job	No go	$45 per day	Go	$55 per day	Go		
Minimum yearly income $10,400	$9,900 per year	No go	$11,700 per year	Go	$14,300 per year	Go		
Maximum commute one hour	30 minute commute	Go	40 minute commute	Go	most work at home/ 45 minute commute	Go		
Must be a "professional" type job	to be considered a profession at least at the company	Go	is at level of professional job	Go	is professional work	Go		

3. OBJECTIVES	4. WT.	8. EVIDENCE	9. EST.	8. EVIDENCE	9. EST.	8. EVIDENCE	9. EST.	8. EVIDENCE	9. EST.
Maximize opportunity for personal and professional growth	10	Chance to learn food processing business	M	Work with good people personally and professionally	M	Not much contact now; terrific contacts if go full time	M		
Maximize compensation	4	Full insurance coverage; paid vacation; retirement plan; good pay schedule	H	Medical insurance; retirement plan; routine pay schedule	M	Benefits high; no benefits part time; full benefits full time	H		
Maximize time with family (2 children in high school)	8	Set work hours; good flextime schedule	M	Some unpredictable night work	L	Could work at home part time; could work on train when commuting	H		
Maximize use of travel in biology	6	Technology will use my background	M	Technology will use my background	M	Draws on my background; will half time be there up in other area	H		
Maximize opportunity for advancement	10	Company committed to advancement of minorities; commitment to EEO	M	Routine advancement	M	Chance of full-time job within a year or so at work	H		
Minimize sexist climate at work	6	People will probably resent females	M	Gov't guidelines followed; don't need so female + being sexist	H	Sensitive people; females accepted	H		
Maximize interest of work	8	Routine at first; can get interesting the more I learn	M	Inspection areas may; work challenging	H	Exposure to wide range of topics	H		
Maximize responsibility for work of its	10	Little responsibility for at first	L	Dept. short-handed I'll get as much responsibility as I can handle	H	I will be an important part of the editorial process, can contribute	M		

10. COMPARE – MAKE TENTATIVE CHOICE

		Fair		Good		Excellent			

11. TEST FOR RISK: WHAT CAN GO WRONG IF I CHOOSE . . . .

	RISK Probability	Seriousness
B ALTERNATIVE _Might lose job for political reasons_	H	H
Tight work might get out of hand	H	H
C ALTERNATIVE _Full-time job may not materialize_	M	M
May not be able to work at home without	M	M
interruptions		
ALTERNATIVE _____		

12. FINAL CHOICE _Alternative B involves too much risk._
Alternative C looks like best opportunity available.

---

5. ALTERNATIVE E _____ 5. ALTERNATIVE F _____ 5. ALTERNATIVE G _____

6. EVIDENCE	7. GO/ NO GO	6. EVIDENCE	7. GO/ NO GO	6. EVIDENCE	7. GO/ NO GO
8. EVIDENCE	9. EST.	8. EVIDENCE	9. EST.	8. EVIDENCE	9. EST.

1. STATEMENT OF DECISION-MAKING SITUATION:	5. ALTERNATIVE A	
TO CHOOSE THE BEST		

2. NONNEGOTIABLE CONSTRAINTS	6. EVIDENCE	7. GO/ NO GO

3. OBJECTIVES	4. WT.	8. EVIDENCE	9. EST
10. COMPARE—MAKE TENTATIVE CHOICE			

5. ALTERNATIVE B		5. ALTERNATIVE C		5. ALTERNATIVE D	
6. EVIDENCE	7. GO/ NO GO	6. EVIDENCE	7. GO/ NO GO	6. EVIDENCE	7. GO/ NO GO
8. EVIDENCE	9. EST.	8. EVIDENCE	9. EST.	8. EVIDENCE	9. EST.

5. ALTERNATIVE E_____		5. ALTERNATIVE F_____		5. ALTERNATIVE G_____	
6. EVIDENCE	7. GO/ NO GO	6. EVIDENCE	7. GO/ NO GO	6. EVIDENCE	7. GO/ NO GO
8. EVIDENCE	9. EST.	8. EVIDENCE	9. EST.	8. EVIDENCE	9. EST.

11. TEST FOR RISK:
WHAT CAN GO WRONG IF I CHOOSE . . .

RISK
Probability   Seriousness

. . . ALTERNATIVE _____

. . . ALTERNATIVE _____

. . . ALTERNATIVE _____

12. FINAL CHOICE_____

Force field
analysis

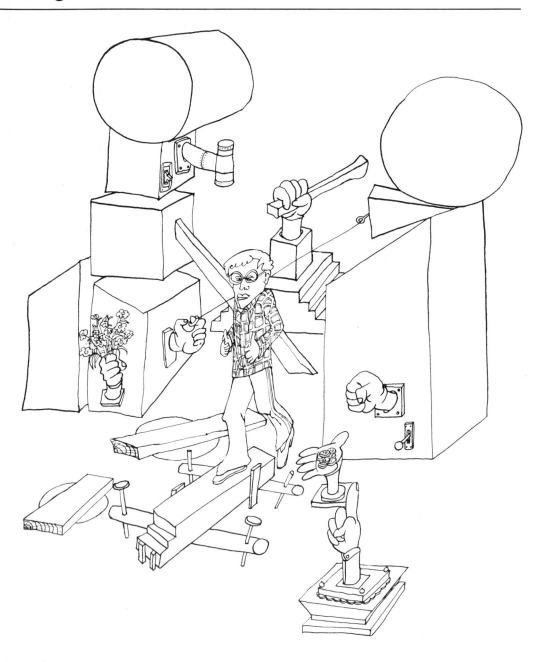

Force Field Analysis is a process for testing the feasibility of a goal or course of action or for planning in personal or interpersonal growth situations. The process enables you to analyze the forces involved in reaching your goal and to set action steps to minimize the negative forces and maximize the positive forces.

Following is a summary of process questions and directions to guide you in each step of the Force Field Analysis work sheet which follows. The questions correspond to numbered steps on the work sheet. Make sure you have answered each question that applies to your situation at each step and recorded your answer on the work sheet. There is an example on pages 164 and 165 to help you get started. If you find that the work sheets do not give you enough room, copy out the headings on a large sheet of paper or on several sheets of paper.

1. *Identify your goal or course of action.* What is the goal or course of action you wish to analyse?

   - State your goal using the word *to* followed by an action verb. Your goal should have a target date.

   - Even if you are undecided and are therefore testing your goal or course of action, formulate it in positive terms. Avoid "Should I or shouldn't I . . . ." and "Whether or not . . . ." formulations.

   - Be specific. Exactly what do you want to accomplish? By when?

   - Check to see whether you have stated more than one goal. A second goal needs separate treatment.

2. *List forces for and against your goal.* What are the forces working for your goal, inside you or outside you? What are the forces working against your goal, inside you or outside you? (*You* may represent a group—a couple, a family, colleagues, etc.).

   - A "force for" is anything that contributes to your reaching your goal. A "force against" is anything that makes it more difficult for you to reach your goal.

   - A reason why you want to do something is not always a "force for."

   - Be very specific. Indicate who, what, where, when, and how much or how many.

   - Indicate the impact each force might have on your goal.

   - The same force can work both for and against your goal. If so, indicate how it does each.

   - Not every positive force will have a corresponding negative force, and vice versa.

   - Do not censor. Brainstorm.

- Get other people's suggestions. List the forces as they occur to you, in no particular order.

3. ***Analyze the forces.*** Which forces seem to you most significant?

   - A force is significant when it is *important* for reaching your goal; when it is certain that it is in fact a *real,* not an assumed force; and when it is *probable* that it will affect your goal. Circle the significant forces.

   - Having poor information means that you do not know how real or important or probable a force is, not that it is not real or unimportant or improbable.

   - Get better information if you need it.

4. ***Actions to maximize positive forces and minimize negative forces.*** What actions can you take to maximize or strengthen positive forces? What actions can you take to minimize, neutralize, overcome, or reverse negative forces?

   - When you set action steps, focus on the forces that are real, important, and probable—the forces you have circled.

   - Be specific about what the action is, who will take it, when, and what resources are needed.

   - You can establish actions to prevent a force from working or to cope with its effect if your preventive action does not work.

   - See if you can set action steps which will change any negative forces into positive forces (for example, give someone more responsibility in order to change low motivation to high motivation).

   - If you cannot establish an action to deal with a force, be sure to note this with a phrase like "No action possible."

   - When you set an action step, indicate by number (1+, 2+, 3+, 1−, 2−, 3−) the force or forces to which the action step refers.

5. ***Assess feasibility of goal.*** Does this goal seem a reasonable one for you?

   - Your goal is feasible if the positive forces clearly outweigh the negative or if your action steps do enough to offset the negative forces.

   - If your goal does seem feasible, take the action steps you have identified.

   - Check to see whether you have a situation to which Project Planning might apply. If you do use Project Planning, you will find that your forces and action steps will recur in the various steps of the planning process.

6. **Forget or adapt goal.** If your goal is not feasible, you have two options: forget about it or adapt. If your option is to adapt, one or more of the following points may be useful:

- Your goal as stated may be too general. Try to make it more specific.

- Your goal as stated may contain more than one goal. If so, break it down into two or more separate goals.

- Your goal may be attainable if you modify it. (If you cannot make manager in two years, try three. If you cannot be a doctor, maybe you can be a medical technician. If you cannot build a perfect relationship, maybe you can build a good one. If something is worth doing, maybe it is worth doing haltingly, rather than not at all.)

- Your real focus may not be your goal at all but a problem or decision which emerges as your central concern. Focus on that.

- Your goal may be somebody else's goal. If so, break out your goal from the goals of other people.

- Your list of forces may really describe a goal other than the one you have stated. If so, identify the goal that best relates to the forces you have listed. You may really be talking about something other than what you think you are concerned with.

PITFALLS IN USING FORCE FIELD ANALYSIS

- Using it where you should be using the planning process. *Planning* implies that you can visualize a set course of action steps laid out in a time sequence.

- Using it in situations which call for comparing alternatives. The process for this is Decision Making.

- Using "Should I or shouldn't I . . . ." or "Whether or not . . . ." formulations to state your goal.

- Being too general about forces.

- Not being specific about how a force will affect your goal.

- Censoring out forces as you list them.

- Working on action steps before you have completed your list of forces and analyzed them for significance.

- Not having enough information to assess whether a force is real, important, or probable.

- Missing ambivalent forces—missing how a force can be both for and against your goal.

FORCE FIELD ANALYSIS

1. GOAL OR COURSE OF ACTION *To become a manager in my company*

   TARGET DATE *2 years*

2. FORCES FOR YOUR GOAL   FORCES AGAINST YOUR GOAL

   1+ *I have high technical competence*
   2+ *My boss, Harold, is retiring in 3 years.*
   3+ *I have a good contact with Josh, a manager who works for Willis.*
   4+ *I am highly motivated.*
   5+ *Business looks good for the company long range.*
   6+ *Pressure is growing for equal opportunity compliance.*
   7+ *I am female. This may open opportunities.*
   8+
   9+
   10+
   11+
   12+
   13+
   14+
   15+
   16+
   17+
   18+
   19+
   20+

   1− *I have little administrative experience.*
   2− *Most people see me as a technical expert.*
   3− *I am female. Some managers, Tom, Hank, and Bill are threatened by this.*
   4− *There is no precedent for a female manager in this company.*
   5− *I am often seen as ambitious and impatient.*
   6− *A management job will be much more demanding of personal time.*
   7−
   8−
   9−
   10−
   11−
   12−
   13−
   14−
   15−
   16−
   17−
   18−
   19−
   20−

3. ANALYZE THE FORCES. CIRCLE THOSE FORCES WHICH ARE *IMPORTANT, REAL,* AND/OR *PROBABLE.*

4. ACTIONS TO MAXIMIZE POSITIVE FORCES AND MINIMIZE NEGATIVE FORCES	WHO	WHEN	RESOURCES
3+, 2- Explain my interest in managing to Willis	Myself, Josh	Lunch next week with J+W	Josh's relationship with Willis
2-, 1- Enroll in management course in business school, evening sessions	Myself	Apply 1 month before next semester	Company's education reimbursement program
3+, 6+ Put pressure on personnel to fill a management job with a female (me)	Myself, Josh, Willis	At lunch after I complete courses	Willis' clout with personnel
5- Enroll in company sponsored communication skills course	Myself	Enroll Monday after performance appraisal	Recommendation from Harold, my performance record
2+ Explain my interest in managing to Harold and get his support and advice	Myself	Performance Appraisal meeting this month	Good relationship with Harold, good performance
2+, 1- Ask Harold for assignment that will give me more responsibility, some managing experience	Myself	"	Good relationship with Harold
5- Try to be more objective and less judgemental in meetings, reports and casual conversations. Ask Sarah for feedback on this	Myself	Start tomorrow, Continue	Sarah

5. ASSESS FEASIBILITY OF GOAL If I can get the support of Willis, the goal seems feasible in this time frame.

6. FORGET OR ADAPT GOAL If not, I may have to move my target date out a year, try another approach, or perhaps look for a manager's position in another company.

FORCE FIELD ANALYSIS

1. GOAL OR COURSE OF ACTION _____

   _____ TARGET DATE _____

2. FORCES FOR YOUR GOAL →   ← FORCES AGAINST YOUR GOAL

   1+ _____   1− _____

   2+ _____   2− _____

   3+ _____   3− _____

   4+ _____   4− _____

   5+ _____   5− _____

   6+ _____   6− _____

   7+ _____   7− _____

   8+ _____   8− _____

   9+ _____   9− _____

   10+ _____   10− _____

   11+ _____   11− _____

   12+ _____   12− _____

   13+ _____   13− _____

   14+ _____   14− _____

   15+ _____   15− _____

   16+ _____   16− _____

   17+ _____   17− _____

   18+ _____   18− _____

   19+ _____   19− _____

   20+ _____   20− _____

3. ANALYZE THE FORCES. CIRCLE THOSE FORCES WHICH ARE *IMPORTANT*, *REAL*, AND/OR *PROBABLE*.

4. ACTIONS TO MAXIMIZE POSITIVE FORCES
   AND MINIMIZE NEGATIVE FORCES   WHO   WHEN   RESOURCES

   _____   _____   _____   _____

   _____   _____   _____   _____

   _____   _____   _____   _____

   _____   _____   _____   _____

   _____   _____   _____   _____

   _____   _____   _____   _____

   _____   _____   _____   _____

   _____   _____   _____   _____

   _____   _____   _____   _____

   _____   _____   _____   _____

   _____   _____   _____   _____

   _____   _____   _____   _____

   _____   _____   _____   _____

   _____   _____   _____   _____

   _____   _____   _____   _____

   _____   _____   _____   _____

   _____   _____   _____   _____

5. ASSESS FEASIBILITY OF GOAL _____

   _____

6. FORGET OR ADAPT GOAL _____

   _____

FORCE FIELD ANALYSIS

1. GOAL OR COURSE OF ACTION _____

   _____ TARGET DATE _____

2. FORCES FOR YOUR GOAL →   ← FORCES AGAINST YOUR GOAL

   1+ _____   1− _____

   2+ _____   2− _____

   3+ _____   3− _____

   4+ _____   4− _____

   5+ _____   5− _____

   6+ _____   6− _____

   7+ _____   7− _____

   8+ _____   8− _____

   9+ _____   9− _____

   10+ _____   10− _____

   11+ _____   11− _____

   12+ _____   12− _____

   13+ _____   13− _____

   14+ _____   14− _____

   15+ _____   15− _____

   16+ _____   16− _____

   17+ _____   17− _____

   18+ _____   18− _____

   19+ _____   19− _____

   20+ _____   20− _____

3. ANALYZE THE FORCES. CIRCLE THOSE FORCES WHICH ARE *IMPORTANT*, *REAL*, AND/OR *PROBABLE*.

4. ACTIONS TO MAXIMIZE POSITIVE FORCES
   AND MINIMIZE NEGATIVE FORCES   WHO   WHEN   RESOURCES

5. ASSESS FEASIBILITY OF GOAL

6. FORGET OR ADAPT GOAL

FORCE FIELD ANALYSIS

1. GOAL OR COURSE OF ACTION _____

_____ TARGET DATE _____

2. FORCES FOR YOUR GOAL →   ← FORCES AGAINST YOUR GOAL

1+ _____	1− _____
2+ _____	2− _____
3+ _____	3− _____
4+ _____	4− _____
5+ _____	5− _____
6+ _____	6− _____
7+ _____	7− _____
8+ _____	8− _____
9+ _____	9− _____
10+ _____	10− _____
11+ _____	11− _____
12+ _____	12− _____
13+ _____	13− _____
14+ _____	14− _____
15+ _____	15− _____
16+ _____	16− _____
17+ _____	17− _____
18+ _____	18− _____
19+ _____	19− _____
20+ _____	20− _____

3. ANALYZE THE FORCES. CIRCLE THOSE FORCES WHICH ARE *IMPORTANT*, *REAL*, AND/OR *PROBABLE*.

4. ACTIONS TO MAXIMIZE POSITIVE FORCES
    AND MINIMIZE NEGATIVE FORCES   WHO   WHEN   RESOURCES

    _____   _____   _____   _____

    _____   _____   _____   _____

    _____   _____   _____   _____

    _____   _____   _____   _____

    _____   _____   _____   _____

    _____   _____   _____   _____

    _____   _____   _____   _____

    _____   _____   _____   _____

    _____   _____   _____   _____

    _____   _____   _____   _____

    _____   _____   _____   _____

    _____   _____   _____   _____

    _____   _____   _____   _____

    _____   _____   _____   _____

    _____   _____   _____   _____

    _____   _____   _____   _____

    _____   _____   _____   _____

    _____   _____   _____   _____

5. ASSESS FEASIBILITY OF GOAL _____

6. FORGET OR ADAPT GOAL _____

Idea building

Idea Building is a process for inventing or improving ideas. It is a carefully structured process that involves starting with one idea and adding to it until it works or until you can see that it just cannot be made to work. It is not the same thing as brainstorming, which is an uninterrupted free flow of ideas and is actually a step in Idea Building.

Your use of Idea Building may be to invent or improve alternatives in Step 5 of Decision Making, to set actions to maximize positive forces or minimize negative forces in Step 4 of Force Field Analysis, or to set action steps to deal with potential problems in Steps 10 and 11 of Project Planning.

Following is a summary of process questions and directions to guide you in each step of the Idea Building work sheet which follows. The questions correspond to numbered steps on the work sheet. Make sure you have answered each question that applies to your situation at each step and recorded your answer on the work sheet. There is a sample on pages 176 and 177 you can refer to. If you find that the work sheets do not give you enough room, copy out the headings on a large sheet of paper or on several sheets of paper.

1. **Situation.** State your situation. Review with your group your Decision Making, Force Field Analysis, or Project Planning work sheets.

2. **Specific problem.** State your problem. Indicate the exact point at which you have a difficulty, an obstacle, or a problem in completing your decision, analysis, or plan. In Decision Making, the problem will be to modify existing alternatives or to invent new ones to meet your objectives. In Force Field Analysis, the problem will be how to maximize a specific positive force or how to minimize a specific negative force. In Project Planning, you will be trying to find out how to prevent and/or cope with specific potential problems.

3. **Ideas to solve your problem—your ideas.** Review the ideas you have for solving your problem. These may include what you have done or thought of doing in the past. Summarize these ideas briefly in a few words on the work sheet, *even if you do not think they will work.*

4. **Others' ideas.** Ask the group to brainstorm ideas to solve your problem. Summarize them briefly in a few words *even if you do not think they will work.* Do not censor. It is essential to write down **every idea,** even if you think it is silly or crazy or comes from a gross misunderstanding of your problem. Any idea can suggest a better one, and censoring breaks the creative flow.

5. **Possible solutions.** Identify any ideas which seem to be obvious solutions to your problem. If you have enough possible solutions, go back to your decision, plan, or analysis or move on to another problem.

6. **Select an idea or approach to work with.** If you want to take the group's time to develop more or better solutions, start by choosing an idea from your list which has some merit or which seems to be a promising approach to solving your problem.

   • Do not record what is said in Steps 7, 8, 9, and 10 until you get to a possible solution, Step 11. If you write down Steps 7 to 10, the process will become slow and tedious. Keep it moving.

   • Do ask the members of your group to write down privately any ideas which they think of and do not get a chance to work in. Have them give these ideas to you at the end of your session so that you can review them for possible use.

7. **Paraphrase.** If you have selected one of your own ideas, repeat it and briefly explain it. If you have selected someone else's idea, paraphrase it. Repeat it back in your own words, checking to see that the sender agrees that you understand what the sender intended to say.

   • Be patient with this step. Repeat the idea as many times as you need to in order to clarify your understanding.

- Be sure you get the whole idea.

- Make sure the sender clarifies the intended meaning of the idea if there is need to.

- Try not to elaborate on the idea as you clarify; just get it straight.

8. *Likes.* State what you like about the idea—its pluses, advantages, what it would do for you.

   - Try to find at least three things you like about the idea. Stretch a little beyond easy and obvious pluses.

   - If you have trouble identifying anything good about the idea, think of yourself as all-powerful and able to implement any idea; what would its advantages be for you if you could do it? *Suspend your judgment.*

9. *Difficulties.* State what you do not like about the idea—its holes, disadvantages, limitations, problems, difficulties, reality constraints—what you wish the idea would do for you that it does not do.

10. *Build.* Ask the group to give you another idea to build on the first one and to fill at least one of its holes. This can be an additional idea or a modification of the first idea, but it must try to make the first idea work and not start an altogether new train of thought.

    - When someone gives you a "build," circle back through Steps 7 (Paraphrase), 8 (Likes), and 9 (Difficulties).

    - If you find that, after several attempts to build on the first idea, the same difficulties keep coming up, try another idea. Don't give up too easily and don't beat a dead horse.

11. *Possible solution.* If there are no difficulties in the idea after the build, write it out as a possible solution. Your group will help you remember any details you miss.

12. If you want additional solutions to your problem, go back through the process until you have enough solutions.

IDEA BUILDING

1. SITUATION _Choose next job situation_

   ☑ DECISION MAKING   CHOICE _Job situation next September_

   ☐ PLANNING   PLAN

   ☐ FORCE FIELD ANALYSIS   GOAL _Will have master's degree in counseling this summer._

   2. SPECIFIC PROBLEM _Want job change like people. Tired of teaching – 5 years experience in high school. Need options. Need ideas._

3. YOUR IDEAS

   Continue to teach same school

   Teach elsewhere

   Try for counselor in present school

   Seek counseling position at other local school

   Move to East Coast – New England, rural post

   Business – personnel position

   Go to Alaska

   State home for delinquents

4. OTHERS' IDEAS

   Government agency

   Work with Headstart

   Get involved in P.E.T. network

   Work with senior citizens

   Peace Corps

   VISTA

   Residential center for teenagers

   Human potential movement

   Work in career counseling

5. POSSIBLE SOLUTIONS

6. SELECT AN IDEA OR APPROACH TO WORK WITH

7. PARAPHRASE

8. LIKES

9. DIFFICULTIES

10. BUILD

Do not write out these steps.

5 and 11. POSSIBLE SOLUTIONS

Join or form private counseling group with my specialty being career counseling, particularly with public schools and churches.

YOU WOULD NOT ACTUALLY WRITE OUT THE FOLLOWING STEPS. THIS IS AN EXAMPLE.

6. SELECT AN IDEA OR APPROACH TO WORK WITH.

Career counseling

7. PARAPHRASE

Get involved in career counseling

8. LIKES

Uses my experience with high school students
Uses my own life experience
Believe that it is very important
Gets me out of the classroom
Is an area now recognized as significant - jobs are available

9. DIFFICULTIES

Need a sharper focus - age, group, employer, location - too general now
My work experience limited to teenagers, teaching
Most likely spot is public high school where patterns of career counseling are often set and very limited

10. BUILD

Find staff position with a community mental health clinic which deals with all age groups - could specialize in teenagers while building broader experience.

7. PARAPHRASE

Get position in community counseling center. Specialize in teenagers now. Build experience with other age groups.

8. LIKES

Is new kind of situation
Continues emphasis on teenagers
Offers small agency/center
Offers opportunity for 1-to-1 counseling

9. DIFFICULTIES

At my best with highly motivated and competent students - community agency often serves drop-outs or people with problems
Community agency of that type generally in larger cities - would really like more rural life

10. BUILD

Join or form private counseling service offering services to broad range of schools, towns, churches, etc., in a larger rural area, to which I could bring my career counseling

7. PARAPHRASE

Get involved with a private consulting firm, mine or another's, in a rural area, with broad client base, where my counseling skills would be an asset

8. LIKES

Builds my own experience - would broaden base
Would keep me in contact with high-school students
My teaching record would be great entree into public schools
Have been active in church groups - interested in service there

9. DIFFICULTIES

Great idea - now only need to find a job! or find a partner.

IDEA BUILDING

1. SITUATION _____

    ☐ DECISION MAKING   CHOICE _____

    ☐ PLANNING   PLAN _____

    ☐ FORCE FIELD ANALYSIS   GOAL _____

2. SPECIFIC PROBLEM _____

3. YOUR IDEAS   4. OTHERS' IDEAS

_____   _____

_____   _____

_____   _____

_____   _____

_____   _____

_____   _____

_____   _____

_____   _____

_____   _____

_____   _____

_____   _____

_____   _____

_____   _____

_____   _____

_____   _____

5. POSSIBLE SOLUTIONS

6. SELECT AN IDEA OR APPROACH TO WORK WITH

7. PARAPHRASE

8. LIKES

9. DIFFICULTIES

10. BUILD

Do not write out these steps.

5 and 11. POSSIBLE SOLUTIONS

IDEA BUILDING

1. SITUATION _____

    ☐ DECISION MAKING   CHOICE _____

    ☐ PLANNING   PLAN _____

    ☐ FORCE FIELD ANALYSIS   GOAL _____

2. SPECIFIC PROBLEM _____

---

3. YOUR IDEAS   4. OTHERS' IDEAS

5.   POSSIBLE SOLUTIONS

6.   SELECT AN IDEA OR APPROACH TO WORK WITH

7.   PARAPHRASE

8.   LIKES

9.   DIFFICULTIES

10. BUILD

Do not write out these steps.

5 and 11.   POSSIBLE SOLUTIONS

IDEA BUILDING

1. SITUATION _____

   ☐ DECISION MAKING   CHOICE _____

   ☐ PLANNING   PLAN _____

   ☐ FORCE FIELD ANALYSIS   GOAL _____

2. SPECIFIC PROBLEM _____

3. YOUR IDEAS   4. OTHERS' IDEAS

_____   _____

_____   _____

_____   _____

_____   _____

_____   _____

_____   _____

_____   _____

_____   _____

_____   _____

_____   _____

_____   _____

_____   _____

_____   _____

_____   _____

5. POSSIBLE SOLUTIONS

6. SELECT AN IDEA OR APPROACH TO WORK WITH

7. PARAPHRASE

8. LIKES

9. DIFFICULTIES

10. BUILD

Do not write out these steps.

5 and 11.   POSSIBLE SOLUTIONS

Appendix

Trend analysis

WHERE ARE YOU TAKING YOURSELF?

WHEN TO USE TREND ANALYSIS

Trend Analysis is a process for taking a close look at your past and present behavior to see where it is taking you and to see what changes you would or would not like to make. It is a diagnostic tool. It might be of use if you are making a major shift and wondering which of your existing values, behaviors, and goals you really want to retain as you move on to new challenges.

HOW TO USE TREND ANALYSIS

Following is a summary of process questions and directions to guide you in each step of the Trend Analysis work sheet which follows. The questions correspond to the numbered steps on the work sheet. Make sure you have answered each question that applies to your situation at each step and recorded your answer on the work sheet.

1. **Values.** What are the items on the checklist that seem important to you? List them and briefly state why they are important (your values). Be as clear as you can.

- Be selective about the items you list. Pick the important ones.

- Values are choices which you cherish, are proud of, are open about, have thought through, have truly chosen from among alternatives, and act on consistently.

2. **Behavior—past and present.** What has been your behavior around each item over the significant past?

- Go back as far as seems useful.

- Use broad strokes and highlight your history without getting bogged down in detail. Yet try to be as specific as is practical.

3. **Behavior trends.** What are the trends in your behavior? Are they toward or away from your values? Consistent or inconsistent with them? Patterned or random? With or without purpose? Positive or negative?

4. **Circumstances.** What are the external conditions or circumstances affecting your behavior? What is the effect?

5. **Projections on behavior.** Given your circumstances, where is your behavior taking you? What is its logical conclusion? Name the payoff or the crisis and set a date for it.

6. **Goals: alternative values, behaviors, or circumstances.** What changes do you wish to make or not make in your values, behavior, or circumstances? What goals (objectives) suggest themselves? What are your next steps from here?

7. **Crossovers.** What are the "crossovers" in your Trend Analysis? Where do behaviors or circumstances around one value have an impact on those around another value?

EXAMPLES

Suppose a value you hold is a strong preference for independent responsibility in your work. Your behavior has been to seek out employment in large organizations. You have held a series of jobs in which there is plenty of responsibility but little real authority. Among your circumstances is a management policy and practice which encourages this split. The trend is one of growing frustration. Projecting, you can see yourself taking one or two years more of this, but then something has to give. A goal emerging from this could be to be in a job with significantly more responsibility and authority within two years.

Or, your value may be to stay in good physical condition. Your behavior has been to spend less and less time in physical activity, more and more in work and socializing. You have gained 6 pounds this year. Circumstances include some friends with common interests, a local club with a gym, a committed social and work schedule, and a flair for gourmet cooking. The overall trend is toward more of the same, and the projection is another 6 pounds, unless you do something drastic and begin to take better advantage of some of the other circumstances in your life. Your goal might be to exercise off the 6 pounds within six months.

Finally, suppose your value is openness with others. Your behavior has been to be pretty closed and defensive, both at home and at work. Recently, you have begun to be less defensive at work and have had some good talks with your spouse and children. You and your spouse have also been involved in a good group experience at church which has given you an opportunity to grow. Circumsta.ices include some new young subordinates at work who are very prone to tell it like it is, and good job security. The projection is for slow, steady growth in the foreseeable future if you are willing to work at it. Goals might be to aim for useful feedback about your openness from your subordinates at the annual appraisal and a significant increase in the amount and quality of your communication with your children.

PITFALLS IN USING TREND ANALYSIS

- Working with only positive or only negative behaviors and trends.

- Being too general.

- Using it to avoid taking action. There comes a time when you have enough information, and you need to act.

- Thinking there is a set sequence to follow in filling out the work sheet. Do what works best. Many people do find it more productive first to fill in column 1, then to work across the page for each separate item on the list rather than vertically down each column.

TREND ANALYSIS

1. VALUES	2. BEHAVIOR—PAST AND PRESENT	3. BEHAVIOR TRENDS
MATERIAL		
PHYSICAL		
EMOTIONAL		
INTELLECTUAL		

4. CIRCUMSTANCES	5. PROJECTIONS ON BEHAVIOR	6. GOALS: ALTERNATIVE VALUES, BEHAVIOR, OR CIRCUMSTANCES

TREND ANALYSIS

1. VALUES	2. BEHAVIOR — PAST AND PRESENT	3. BEHAVIOR TRENDS
OCCUPATIONAL		
SPIRITUAL		
SOCIAL		
OTHER		

4. CIRCUMSTANCES	5. PROJECTIONS ON BEHAVIOR	6. GOALS: ALTERNATIVE VALUES, BEHAVIOR, OR CIRCUMSTANCES

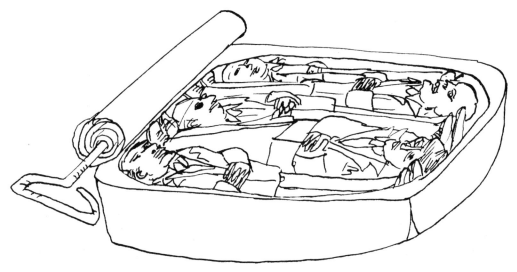

Redefining your work

WHO NEEDS YOU?

This activity is a device for (1) defining the scope of your present work activities, (2) diagnosing your effectiveness within it, (3) increasing your effectiveness, and/or (4) thinking beyond the present scope of your work. (You might also apply this to your free time or social life.)

Your effectiveness is defined by the relation between what you do and why you do it. If what you do—your activities (products and/or services)—produces the clearly defined results you had in mind, you are being effective. (On occasion, you may be lucky enough to produce good results which you did not intend.)

The idea behind this activity is a well-known marketing concept. Product development should start not with a product idea but with a market need. It is generally more effective to identify needs or markets first and then fashion what you do or make to respond to these needs. This is a better approach than to develop something and then hope you will find a need or market.

This activity seems to be most productive in situations where you see or think you see some hope for improvement, growth, or advancement in your present situation. If the situation turns out to be hopeless, the last step in this activity takes you beyond the present situation.

1. **Products/services.** First, select the work situation that you wish to analyze for effectiveness. It may be a specific job or work situation, schoolwork, household or family work, or volunteer work. State your situation briefly in the space at the top of the work sheet below.

   Now think of yourself as a minicorporation or enterprise—the John Brown Company or the Mary Brown Company. Consider your activities as products and/or services that people buy from you. If you work for an organization, your buyers may be inside or outside that organization.

   In column 1, make a list of your current activities, your tasks, how you spend your time. These are the *products* and/or *services* which you are now marketing, what you *make* and/or *do* in your present situation, what people buy from your minicorporation.

   Select the minimum time period—a day, week, month, assignment, project, semester, quarter, half year, year, season, etc.— which best represents the full range of your activities.

   Make a rough estimate of how much *time* (hours, days, percentage of time per cycle) you spend during that period on each of the items on your list and record your estimate next to each item on your list.

2. **Market.** Now, in column 2, make a list of who makes up your market, *who* it is who needs what you do and/or make—your boss, your peers, managers in other departments or divisions, outside customers, children, family, friends, etc. Be specific (instead of naming "management," name the manager or managers by name). Who is your market?

   Next, opposite each "who," make a list of *what* is the specific *need* your activity (product or service) fills. Why does each person on your list need (or want or buy) your products and/or services from you? Why are you doing what you are doing? What results do you intend to achieve? What are your objectives? If nobody needs you, better you find this out and do something about it than that your manager or someone else find out and does something about it.

3. **New markets.** If you are doing this activity with a group, share with each other what you have written in columns 1 and 2. The following points may be useful for reflection and/or sharing:

   Where are you on your "who" list? If you are completely absent from it, you might raise a question about how your activities are meeting your personal needs. If you dominate your list, you might raise a question about how useful you are to your organization or to others around you. Some sort of balance between these two is generally appropriate. The ideal balance produces synergy, which results when you achieve your own goals best by achieving the goals of your organization, family, or group.

   Is the scope of your present work satisfactory? Do your activities, objectives, or the needs you meet give you enough responsibility, room for achievement, personal and professional growth, recognition, interest, horizon for advancement, monetary reward, satisfactory relationships with others?

If the scope of your work is satisfactory, you might want to explore how *effective* you are in your work. Is the relation between what you do and why you do it sufficiently clear? Can you make more effective use of your time? Can you cut some of the losers, the fat, the useless and low-priority activities?

If you want to increase your effectiveness, concentrate on refining the relationship between what you do and why you do it.

4. ***New products/services.*** If you want to extend, develop, or change the scope of your work, there are several options open to you:

    •   Hold to your present range of products and/or services and the needs they meet, but find more people who have these needs. Extend your list of "whos." Find out who *else* has the same need for the same product and/or service you offer. (They'll love it in Cincinnati!) Record these new "whos" in column 3 under "Who *else* needs what you do/make?"

    •   Hold to your present market—your present clients or the persons you serve—and see if they have any new needs you might also fill. (They needed financial accountability from you; maybe they also need financial planning.) This may make it necessary for you to respond with products and/or services beyond your present ones. Write down the new needs in column 3, under "*new* needs." Write down *new products/services* to meet these needs in column 4.

    •   Scrap your present products and/or services and market and strike out on a new venture. Divest and diversify. This is a more radical alternative than the previous two. It involves moving into a second (or third, etc.) career, a major shift. It involves developing a new market, with *new needs* and *new products and/or services* to meet them. Write down what you can about this new venture in columns 3 and 4. If you have trouble identifying new options, try the Newspaper Exercise or Idea Building.

Be sure to leave room for common sense and serendipity, luck and miracles. Some skills or inventions are worth finding a market for.

REDEFINING YOUR WORK

YOUR WORK SITUATION

1. PRODUCTS/SERVICES
What you DO/MAKE

TIME

2. MARKET:
WHO needs what you do/make?

WHAT is the NEED?

NEW needs

TIME

3. NEW MARKETS
WHO ELSE needs
what you do/make?

4. NEW PRODUCTS/SERVICES
HOW can you meet new needs?

The newspaper exercise

WHAT DO YOU SEE?

For this activity, you will need a copy of a major city daily newspaper for each (*The New York Times* is very good for this), a felt pen or crayon for each, and the work sheet below. You can use other sources of information in this activity: local newspapers, periodicals, or magazines (*The Wall Street Journal, Time,* etc.) or data about available employment opportunities. Make sure your sources are broadly based and cover a wide spectrum of topics. You may wish to select publications which reflect a geographical area or an area of special interest — trade or industry publications.

This activity is designed to broaden present work involvement or invent new alternatives. It makes the same marketing assumption made by the preceding activity: The best way to innovate products and services is first to define your market and its needs.

It also assumes that most problems are symptoms of unresolved social needs. If the needs in problems can be identified, then problems stand a chance of being translated into opportunities to which you can respond with marketable products or services.

1. ***Present situation: why you are looking for alternatives.*** State your present situation and indicate why you are looking for alternatives.

2. **Problems.** Scan the newspaper for 20 minutes. (More time will give more data.) Look for items anywhere in the paper (ads and pictures included) which you think indicate *problems* of specific interest to yourself or other members of your group today, problems to which you or others might personally respond—not global, general problems. Circle the items in the paper, indicate whose interest you have in mind, formulate the problems briefly and specifically, and enter them on the work sheet below. If you identify *other items* of interest, circle them as well and list them in column 2.

3. **Needs and opportunities.** When you reach 10 items or when time is up, list in column 3 the unfulfilled social *needs* of which each problem is the symptom. Specify exactly *what* the need is and *who* has it. There may be more than one need and more than one "who" for any given problem.

4. **Products and/or services.** Next, probe to see if any need opens up an **opportunity** for you or someone else to respond with a specific *product* or *service*. Not every need will. See if you can respond to the market you have identified. Your response might go beyond a specific product and/or service and develop into a plan, project, program, or strategy. Record your findings in column 4.

Next, meet with your group and share the lists. Work on areas that promise to be fruitful for individuals in your group rather than on those that are merely interesting or controversial. Be sure to point out to others the items you think might be of interest to them.

THE NEWSPAPER EXERCISE

1. PRESENT SITUATION: WHY ARE YOU LOOKING FOR ALTERNATIVES? _____

2. PROBLEMS	3. NEEDS	4. PRODUCTS/SERVICES
	What is the need?	
	Who has the need?	

Bibliography

Bach, George, and Peter Wyden: *The Intimate Enemy,* Morrow, New York, 1969.

Berne, Eric: *Games People Play,* Grove Press, New York, 1964.

Bolles, Richard Nelson: *What Color Is Your Parachute? (A Practical Manual for Job-Hunters and Career-Changers*), Ten Speed Press, Berkeley, Calif., 1972.

Crystal, John C., and Richard N. Bolles: *Where Do I Go From Here with My Life?* Seabury, New York, 1974.

Glasser, William: *Reality Therapy,* Harper & Row, New York, 1965.

Gordon, Thomas: *Parent Effectiveness Training,* Peter U. Wyden, New York, 1970.

Greenwald, Jerry: *Be the Person You Were Meant to Be,* Dell, New York, 1974.

Harris, Thomas A.: *I'm OK—You're OK,* Harper & Row, New York, 1967.

Herzberg, Frederick: "One More Time: How Do You Motivate Employees?" *Harvard Business Review,* January–February 1968.

James, Muriel, and Dorothy Jongeward: *Born to Win,* Addison-Wesley, Reading, Mass., 1971.

Jung, C. G.: *The Undiscovered Self,* Mentor Books, New York, 1957.

Kepner, Charles, and Benjamin Trejoe: *The Rational Manager,* McGraw-Hill, New York, 1965.

Kübler-Ross, Elisabeth: *Death: The Final Stage of Growth,* Prentice Hall, Englewood Cliffs, N.J., 1975.

————: *On Death and Dying,* Macmillan, New York, 1969.

————: *Questions and Answers on Death and Dying,* Macmillan, New York, 1974.

LeShan, Eda: *The Wonderful Crisis of Middle Age,* Warner Paperback Library, New York, 1974.

Loring, Rosalind K., and Herbert A. Otto: *New Life Options (The Working Woman's Resource Book),* McGraw-Hill, New York, 1976.

Maslow, Abraham H.: *Eupsychian Management,* Dorsey-Irwin, Homewood, Ill., 1965.

————: *The Farther Reaches of Human Nature,* Penguin, Baltimore, 1971.

————: *Motivation and Personality,* Harper & Row, New York, 1954.

————: *Toward a Psychology of Being,* Van Nostrand, Princeton, N.J., 1962.

Newman, Mildred, and Bernard Berkowitz: *How to Take Charge of Your Life,* Harcourt Brace Jovanovich, New York, 1977.

———— and ————: *How to be Your Own Best Friend,* Ballantine Books, New York, 1974.

O'Neill, Nena, and George O'Neill: *Shifting Gears,* Avon, New York, 1974.

Otto, Herbert A.: *Group Methods to Actualize Human Potential,* Holistic Press, Beverly Hills, Calif., 1968.

———— and John Mann: *Ways of Growth,* Pocket Books, New York, 1971.

Perls, Frederick S.: *Gestalt Therapy Verbatim,* Real People Press, Lafayette, Calif., 1969.

Prince, George M.: *The Practice of Creativity,* Collier Books, New York, 1970.

Raths, Louis E., Merrill Harmin, and Sidney B. Simon: *Values and Teaching,* Merrill, Columbus, Ohio, 1966.

Rogers, Carl R.: *On Becoming a Person,* Houghton Mifflin, Boston, 1961.

Schutz, William C.: *Here Comes Everybody,* Harper & Row, New York, 1971.

————: *Joy,* Grove Press, New York, 1967.

Simon, Sidney B.: *Meeting Yourself Halfway,* Argus Communications, Niles, Ill., 1974.

————, Leland W. Howe, and Howard Kirschenbaum: *Values Clarification,* Hart Publishing, New York, 1972.

Toffler, Alvin: *Future Shock,* Random House, New York, 1970.

Watts, Alan W.: *The Book,* Collier Books, New York, 1966.